# The
# American
# Business
# System

A HISTORICAL PERSPECTIVE · 1900–1955

*The Library of Congress Series
in American Civilization
Edited by
Ralph Henry Gabriel*

HC106
C638

# The American Business System

## A HISTORICAL PERSPECTIVE · 1900–1955

### Thomas C. Cochran
University of Pennsylvania

## HARVARD UNIVERSITY PRESS

Cambridge, Massachusetts

1960

JAN 1965

94768

© *Copyright 1957 by the President and Fellows of Harvard College*

*Distributed in Great Britain by Oxford University Press, London*

*Second Printing*

*Library of Congress Catalog Card Number 57–12964*

*Printed in the United States of America*

# *Foreword*

**W**ell-accepted general theories regarding the operation and control of the American economic system at mid-century are lacking. A usual recourse in such a situation is to seek help from history. But economic history has slighted the importance of the institutions of business and the role of entrepreneurship in over-all developments, while there has been too little general writing about these latter elements to establish a rival pattern for analyzing United States economic growth. For better understanding, a new and broader synthesis is needed. The present book attempts to put the closely related factors together in a new balance, to see the history of business forms and business action in their essential relationships to technological and industrial change, and to suggest some of the interactions of the whole complex with the rest of American civilization.

Important antecedents to the present situation began to emerge clearly around the end of the last century. Oil, electricity, chemistry, and the gasoline engine introduced a new technology; new corporate and financial practices created modern big business and big banking; and government increased its regulation and support of economic activity. The ensuing half-century has been a period of the adjustment of these forces to each other and to American society, sometimes tolerably successful, but never with a true promise of stability. Even the mid-century plateau of high prosperity is based on a level of military expenditure justifiable only in an upset world. By seeing how the present structure came to be, layer by layer, as investment bankers, corporate entrepreneurs, political leaders, and the ubiquitous technicians made their contributions, one may better estimate the relative permanence and force of the various elements.

Since this book is one in a series on twentieth-century American civilization, in which there are separate volumes on farmers and organized labor, discussion of these groups will be held to the minimum necessary for an understanding of their relation to other business and economic factors. The basis for inclusion in this brief interpretation for general readers has been the essential character of a development, at some period, as a factor in changing economic institutions.

The forbidding sound of such terms as "system," or "economically oriented institutional change," calls attention to the lack of an adequate vocabulary. The term "economic" has come in practice to refer to trends and activities potentially measurable, and "business" to different readers means various things, of which the greatest common denominator might be a social institution for creating and distributing goods and services for profit. There is no term except "capitalism" for the system as a whole, and capitalism like socialism is loaded with historical meaning that confuses present analysis. This predicament has prompted the choice of "business" as the generic term for the interrelationships of men and machines that have led to socio-economic change.

On occasion this choice necessitates characterizing the whole economic system as American business, or speaking of an industry as a type of business. Aside from the justification that no other generic term seems more satisfactory, business denotes the human activity whereby underlying change is given social effect, and redresses an underemphasis on culture and an overemphasis on impersonal forces in conventional economic history.

One cause of increasing difficulty in defining or even visualizing economically induced social or cultural change is that each new stage of production and business organization has failed to obliterate older forms, but has instead been superimposed on them. Thus mid-twentieth-century America may be seen as having at least three or four partly distinct business systems. There is a section composed of small enterprises in industry, service, and trade that has not changed radically in its organization since the nineteenth century, and this segment contains by far the largest number of businessmen. There is an area of medium-sized and big business that is reasonably free from government control of its operations, while there is another area of such business that is strictly regulated and quite dependent on government policy. And then there is the interaction of these partly conflicting elements in a general and recognizable American system.

The ensuing discussion takes up those ingredients of the system that appear to have been most dynamic at various periods and groups them in separate chapters. Among such major ingredients have been technology, which sets the potential forms and levels of production, the operation of manufacturing industry that accounts for the vast flow of products, the amount of saving and the channels of investment, the character of businessmen and business institutions, the rise of the "welfare state," and changing conceptions of the social place and responsibilities of business. In accord with this plan, areas such as wholesale trade which have not been key elements in change are not discussed, whereas investment banking is emphasized because of its dynamic role in the period before 1929; or again, much routine history of transportation and industry is omitted while changes in national income and its distribution are described as important elements in the development of the mid-century system. In discussing the ingredients of change, it is logical and convenient to divide the period since 1900 into two parts. Up to the collapse of 1929 older beliefs in the self-regulating character of the economy, and the corollary of limited government action, tended to separate political and economic activity. From the thirties on, these two activities were drawn rapidly together in the modern centralized, militarized, and welfare-directed state.

The ablest thinkers cannot agree on how to characterize the whole, where it is headed, or how it will operate in crises. The combination of the vast American productivity, the intricate relations of widely dispersed private ownership with both management and government, the increasingly high standard of living, and the leadership of a group of college-educated professional managers has not existed before and is not duplicated elsewhere in the world. Probably this new complex is more stable than the old-style pre-1929 capitalism. Certainly its stability is of vastly more concern to the rest of the world than ever before. This book aims to provide knowledge of the operation of the American system in the recent past with the hope that better understanding will improve the future prospects of economic stability, democracy, and human welfare.

The facts and interpretations presented come from some thirty years of research in the history of American business. Documentation is mainly limited to the conventional indication of the source of direct quotations. To give credit to others' research, the source that called my attention to a statement rather than the original publication is frequently cited. General documentation of facts and conclusions is in some cases impossible and in others too cumbersome for such a volume. The former difficulty arises because a considerable amount of information comes from confidential sources that I have agreed not to quote, and the latter from the multiplicity of sources that often lie back of a simple generalization. These are the usual problems in presenting analyses that have been derived partly from interviews with the actors themselves or with their close associates, and partly from living through the experience. If occasionally material is drawn from some little-known but readily available source, the fact will be noted.

In addition to a subsidy from the Library of Congress, the research for this book was facilitated by grants from the American Philosophical Society and the University of Pennsylvania. With the permission of Harvard University Press and the Library of Congress the gist of the final chapter was published in the *Harvard Business Review* for March-April 1956. Arthur H. Cole and William Miller read the manuscript and made useful suggestions. Rosamond B. Cochran helped in a wide variety of ways. I wish to thank them and also Ralph H. Gabriel, the Editor of this series.

Thomas C. Cochran

# Contents

# Part One

1900–1930

# 1

## Business as an American Institution

The effectiveness of businessmen in guiding economic development depends to a large degree upon the place
occupied by business in the national culture. If other occupations have more prestige and other values more force, the
ablest members of society are going to be drawn away from
business, and business plans are going to be uneconomically
modified to conform to the dominant values. A logical point
of departure for a study of the business system, therefore, is
the place of business institutions in society.

If the term "businessman" is used to designate anyone who
participates in decisions for organizing the production and
distribution of goods and services for profit, there are many
kinds of American businessmen. Some work behind the count-
ers of small shops, others in grimy, cluttered offices in the
corners of factories, and still others in handsomely furnished
suites. Some businesses have been run in much the same way
for generations and have altered but little between 1900 and
mid-century; others have been forced into continuous adjustment to meet changes in technology. The man in the luxurious
office is likely to be there because mass-production machinery,
efficient transportation, and a broad market necessitate big,
highly capitalized business. The man behind the counter mir-
rors the fact that no electric brain has yet eliminated the
human proprietor from retailing or service.

As used here, "businessman" includes an indefinite fringe of
policy-making executives, but as in defining most social groups,

1

precision is impossible. Even by this broad description most Americans of the twentieth century have not been businessmen. Scarcely one American family in six, in 1900 or even later, had a member who ran a business or occupied an important managerial position. Working in a business company might subtly condition the lower-level employee to business folkways and beliefs, but it did not make him a businessman in either his own or the public's estimation. Although to foreigners America was a land of business, to Americans businessmen were a group apart.

### THE BUSINESS HERITAGE

Compared with the businessmen of other nations, those of America have always had unusual social prestige. Even in the seventeenth and eighteenth centuries, when the manorial lords of great estates on the rivers and bays had formed the traditional elite, merchants in the seaports had been able to attain high social rank. In Charleston, South Carolina, center of a proud plantation aristocracy, planters apprenticed their younger sons and married their daughters to the men of the counting houses. The status of merchant generally rose still higher as one went north until on the seacoast of New England the social supremacy of the great merchant was unquestioned.

In spite of the plans of kings or proprietors, the forms of feudalism were never securely fastened on the American colonies, and there were no lasting titles based on landed estates. Since Great Britain garrisoned the colonies and appointed the chief civil servants, army and government careers were either closed or less attractive to Americans than would have been the case in an independent nation. The Church of England had no American bishops, and the other churches tolerated in the colonies were nonhierarchical. Only in New England did great prestige attach to the ministry. Even here the prestige was diminishing by the end of the colonial period.

In the struggle for social eminence, therefore, the businessman did not have to face strong and repressive competition from titled nobility, army, navy, government, or church. Business and the businesslike profession of the law were in general the broadest and shortest avenues to financial success and public recognition. Whereas in Great Britain the title of barrister, attorney, or merchant was looked down upon by the aristocracy, in America each of these carried social prestige in itself, the title of merchant generally being reserved for men of large affairs in overseas trade.

By the close of the Civil War the prestige of the land had waned in the metropolitan circles that dominated American society, and no new occupations had arisen seriously to threaten the leadership of business and the law. For some years after the war the title of general carried weight, but the army shrank to a garrison for strategic seaports and Indian posts and the hundred days of the Spanish-American War produced no new great generals to perpetuate *la gloire militaire*. The ministry and the learned professions grew in numbers but scarcely in social prestige, and practitioners of the arts, other than journalism or literature, were, to say the least, not widely acclaimed.

The power of the pen was not to be neglected as a source of social control or political or economic position. But increasingly this power was wielded by and for business. Literary men in the service of trade, following the lead of Thomas Paine, rationalized in books and articles the needs of corporations or industries. At the top levels of metropolitan journalism the distinctions between the publisher's functions as a big businessman and those as a purveyor of news were by 1900 becoming blurred.

Only the age-old and inveterate rival of the businessman, the politician, remained strong. The exact balance in prestige between business and politics in America of 1900 is difficult to determine, but perhaps it need not be struck. Of national politicians in the decade 1900 to 1910, selected in a study by William Miller as the most important, over 30 per cent had been or were in business or business law as well as in politics.[1] Furthermore, the personal wealth that successful politicians possessed was often invested in business ventures rather than in land. Consequently, while individual politicians might seek favor with the voters by supporting acts not favored by most businessmen, political leaders as a social group had no desire to lessen the power or prestige of business.

## COMPETING VALUES AND IDEALS

While business values and attitudes were developed and accepted by a large part of the upper classes or social elite, the mass of the people gave only a grudging acceptance to the business system as represented in the careers of "masters of capital" and "captains of industry." Boys and young men were taught at home and in school to seek success, but were also advised that there were spiritual values superior to money-making. "The supreme vice of commercialism," said Bishop Potter in 1902, "is that it is without an ideal." [2] This statement, made to an assembly of Yale students, illustrates the unwillingness of the Bishop, and no doubt other clergymen, to accept the validity of ideals less spiritual than those of the church. He failed to recognize the goal of a higher standard of living as an "ideal" of commerce adhered to implicitly by most Americans. A generation after the Bishop's statement an astute French observer called the American standard of living "a sacred acquisition . . . in which they will allow no reduction, and which they will defend to the uttermost against both competition and surreptitious invasion of other countries." [3] Henry Ford saw the increasing standard of living as leading to new and better ways of life, "contributing something deep and lasting." The authors of *The American Business Creed* aptly term Ford's view the "spiritualization of material progress." [4] "Commercialism" or business was the source and protector of the rising standard of living, and hence shared in its "sanctity."

Yet many persons regarded business as unscrupulous, undemocratic, and materialistic. The paradox resulted in part from the distinction between "commercialism" or capitalism as a way of life, an approved social system, and "business" as a particular institution within the system through which a minority group controlled production and distribution.

No culture can be satisfactorily characterized by a single

phrase. Yet businesslike values and respect for them seemed the most pervasive common element in American culture, more so than religion, world mission, the democratic spirit, or similar formulations of American ideals. Of the primary business belief that the American way rested on the chance for any able individual to gain wealth, Ralph H. Gabriel writes: "This faith and philosophy became the most persuasive siren in American life. It filled the highways with farm boys trekking to the city. It drained the towns and countryside of Europe. It persuaded the educated young man that the greatest rewards in life were to be found in the business world. It taught the ambitious that power lies in wealth rather than in political office. It penetrated the workshop and paralyzed the effort of the labor leader undertaking a crusade for justice to the working man." [5]

The business philosophy reinforced earlier Protestant ethics stemming from Calvinism. Now become partly secular, these beliefs had emphasized the importance of choosing a proper calling, of doing one's appointed task, and of success as a sign of God's grace. A part of the frontier environment had also emphasized success through business enterprise and planning for a future always expected to surpass the present. The Calvinist and frontier traditions had been absorbed in the business life of thousands of country towns and small cities whose citizens strongly influenced the surrounding countryside. Even in the farming areas Lewis Atherton writes of "the mingled fear, distrust, and respect with which citizens regarded the small circle of leaders in frontier towns." [6]

The ambiguous position of business as such is reflected in attitudes toward its leaders. People of the upper intellectual levels gloried in the strength that prodigious economic development gave to the nation, extolled the American system of individual initiative, competition, and material success, but refused to acclaim business leaders as the topmost representatives of the culture. A magazine writer in 1902 noted that "when the prince of one of the reigning houses . . . came to explore somewhat in the Strenuous Land, it was . . . the captains of industry he most desired to meet . . . Yet, for the most part these men's records are to be found in no dictionary of American biography; many are not in 'Who's Who?'; they figure but little in the columns of the press; they are not the types that have been chosen to stand for American greatness in the Hall of Fame." [7]

Americans of 1900 who collectively typified business culture to foreigners, and who, if we had means to measure, may in reality have been chiefly conditioned by this omnipresent environment, obviously thought of themselves as primarily representing other qualities. They liked Teddy Roosevelt's emphasis on "the fundamental qualities of courage, honesty and common sense." [8] They dramatized themselves as part of an inevitably conquering Anglo-American civilization, or as the leaders of democracy in the world, or as God's chosen instrument for creating the perfect society. One might say that the business habits and values were so much a part of the American scene that to natives they were taken for granted as part of the normal order.

Yet these habits and values with their emphasis on saving, investment, and efficient work were far from usual in the rest of the world. While every society has "saved" part of its income, the ends for which income is saved or spent have taken many forms. The Tibetans, for example, although miserably poor, invested hundreds of thousands of hours of their labor in weaving the largest banner in the world to hang on an outer wall of the Portala, the Dalai Lama's residence in Lhasa. In general, static class-bound agricultural societies showed little tendency to invest in tools for further production, except for the amounts necessary to keep existing equipment in repair. The rich of many nations of Asia, Africa, and South America preferred to spend their income in London or Paris rather than to save for investment at home. The people of these countries viewed work as a necessary evil and would have found it hard to understand Henry Ford's belief that "thinking men know that work is the salvation of the race, morally, physically, socially. Work does more than get us our living; it gets us our life." [9]

## THE IMPORTANCE OF SMALL BUSINESS

In his famous "Cross of Gold" speech at the Democratic Convention of 1896 William Jennings Bryan specifically mentioned the "crossroads merchant" as part of the group oppressed by Wall Street businessmen. Yet a count of businessmen would show them to be chiefly crossroads or corner-store merchants, small manufacturers, or distributors. It has been the position and prestige of this latter group in society that has probably been most important in making America a business culture. These were the men who were active in all town affairs. Their buildings gave the town form and character. For their own ends, if no other, they improved the streets and formed civic bodies. No manor houses in the surrounding countryside overshadowed their residences, no country gentry dictated the tone and temper of local affairs. This was business "democracy."

It was probably misleading even by 1900 to call back-country Americanism a "grass-roots" culture. "The history of the Middle Border," says Atherton, "has been largely the history of its towns." [10] The middle- or upper-class townspeople were the ones who had the business folkways and mores, and who spoke for society in both praise and criticism of business. William Allen White, "Sage of Emporia," Kansas, notes many times in his autobiography that his businessman father belonged, because of his success, to the ruling class. "I knew definitely and with conscious pride that I belonged to the governing class . . . We were the people." [11] Local politics were largely run by the merchants, manufacturers, and lawyers, and the same group directed the charities, schools, and clubs. "Every country town," according to Atherton, "had an inner circle whose own personal interests were so tightly woven with those of the community at large that one cannot determine where self-interest ended and public spirit began." [12] The newspaper publisher, large or small, was a member of this local business group. The opinions of this group were most often expressed in print, because in the eyes of the publisher they represented "ordinary common sense."

If attention is turned to a social elite, to the small fraction of the population which gets ahead and assumes social leadership, it might be more fitting to speak of a shop- or desk-rooted culture. Of Miller's 334 men systematically chosen to represent the topmost business and political elite of the first decade of the present century, only fifty had fathers who were farmers; only four, moreover, had fathers who could be classed as "workers." [13]

### THE OPPONENTS OF BUSINESS

How then did it happen that at the end of a century of massive physical achievement by entrepreneurs, "business" came under a mounting attack from the general public and its political representatives? One answer was that employees did not identify their personal interests with those of the companies for which they worked. Another was that in the nineties farmers were still numerous, depressed socially and economically, but well organized and favored politically by geographical representation. In varying ways farmers thought themselves both exploited and despised by businessmen. Many of them hoped that government regulation or ownership could curb such exploitation.

But these are only partial answers to the question. When hostile critics used the word "business" they generally meant big, corporate business. The political influence of such business was evident in the pressures of the big corporations or trade associations upon state capitals or upon Washington. Representative Mills of Texas had said in 1894 that the emasculation of Cleveland's effort at tariff reduction posed the question whether this was a government of the people, or one of taxation by trusts and monopolies. The Bryan campaign of 1896 abounded with charges that business controlled the government and had bought the Cleveland administration, lock, stock, and barrel.

Furthermore, on most specific political measures business was arrayed against itself: a few entrepreneurs were able to build trusts, a larger group of small enterprises wanted trusts curbed; manufacturers usually lobbied for tariffs, the railroads opposed protective duties; manufacturers might favor slum improvement, the local real-estate group fought the necessary regulations. The debates of the late nineties in Congress were not so much concerned with the issues of individualism against collectivism as those of small business against large.

✗ Business as a whole seldom came under attack, even from the farmers. Bryan said approvingly: "The man who is employed for wages is as much a businessman as his employer"; the wage earner asked only for equal opportunities.[14] The Populists, the most radical agrarian party of the late nineteenth century, wanted government ownership of some of the utilities that served the farmer, but only government aid for the free enterprise of commercial farming. Few people attacked what an anthropologist might regard as the central themes of the business culture. Such elements as belief in the virtue of labor, particularly for those lacking in material goods; the importance of material success; the obligation of men to work for a higher general standard of living; the idea that competition was good within "reasonable" limits — all these were accepted by both critics and defenders of specific business or industrial practices.

Such criticisms as there were of the central business values came from a few spiritual or intellectual leaders and a scarcely larger number of extreme radicals. In spite of the protests of Bishop Potter and other clergymen, the age-old challenge to renounce the things of this world and live only for God was muted; it had in fact seldom been emphasized in nineteenth-century Protestantism. Quite generally God was assumed to approve of material progress and the higher standard of living, and therefore God's work and one's own could be regarded as the same. Social welfare rather than metaphysical considerations increasingly provided doctrine for the churches.

Henry and Brooks Adams, as well as William Graham Sumner, thought, for different reasons, that the society was decaying, but the elder Adams and Sumner had no program for reform. The native Marxian labor leaders, such as Debs and de Leon, denounced capitalists and exploitation, but only because they held socialism a better way for achieving the same material ends. Even the philosophical anarchists had swung away from the old "simple life" conception of Bronson Alcott or Robert Dale Owen toward dreams of a highly productive industrial society controlled by workingmen's syndicates.

The nationalists, such as Albert Beveridge, John Hay, and Theodore Roosevelt, influenced among others by Brooks Adams, attacked the existing order from an angle that presaged some of the shifts in opinion of the mid-twentieth century. To them the elements of the "business culture" should be secondary to the fact that Americans were a "conquering race." Continuing this argument Beverdige proclaimed: "We must obey our blood and occupy new markets and if necessary new lands." [15] On another occasion he besought "an English-speaking peoples' league of God for the permanent peace of this war-torn world." [16] Roosevelt said: "No national life is worth having if the nation is not willing to stake everything on the supreme arbitrament of war, and to pour out its blood, its treasure, and tears like water rather than to submit to the loss of honor and renown." [17]

Here were a set of cultural beliefs not included in the Calvinist-frontier-business complex — beliefs that had temporarily intruded before, to be sure, but were not part of the everyday cultural patterns. As implied in Beveridge's phrases "obey our blood and occupy new markets," these nationalistic beliefs were not directly antibusiness. The *necessary* business values could have their cultural niche, as in imperial Germany, but the nation, in Roosevelt's words, should not be dominated by "men with the souls of glorified pawnbrokers." [18] The business virtues and values should be secondary. World War II and the transformation of the United States into a heavily armed military nation were to pose this conflict in values much more seriously.

### THE RISE OF MANAGERIAL ENTERPRISE

In the twentieth century forces within the complex that we have called business culture were to bring about changes in practice, if not always in belief, as striking as those caused by the rise of the military virtues and the mid-century sense of world insecurity. Most of these inner changes can be seen as reactions to changing technology. The one to be noted at this point is that large-scale mass production and transportation hastened the shift toward managerial rather than proprietary control of business enterprise.

As business corporations rapidly became larger, a new type of businessman rose to leadership: the professional executive. In contrast to the smaller business firm run by its owners, the new big companies placed executive control in the hands of careerists, selected for their managerial ability. The professional executive needed to own no stock in the enterprise, and if he did buy some it was usually not enough to give him any great stake in the company profits. In railroads, public utilities, and the new industrial "trusts," ownership was usually distributed among thousands of stockholders, and neither stock nor wealth were necessary qualifications for managerial office.

The resulting split between ownership and control altered business aims and motives. An early fear of loss of initiative and enterprise in such a system, expressed by a prominent professional executive, was that "the average man will not work as closely for the railroad company as he will for himself." [19] But the problem went much deeper than closeness or diligence of work. The profit motive itself, the initial dynamo of capitalism, became altered, and security and personal prestige assumed new importance. The directors of a corporation asked of their employees devotion to duty, loyalty, and co-operation in a hierarchy rather than rational hedonism in a market.

Looked at from the outside, the executive of the large corporation came to play a different social role from that of the owner-manager of a smaller competitive business. The professional executive's horizons were expected to be broader than those of the small businessman; he should see business problems in longer range and in their social setting; he should employ specialists to advise him on the probable results of his decisions; he should be the guardian of jobs and savings and the supplier of utilities to thousands of people; he should be a planner seeking to thwart uncertainty by better control of the market. In spite of his free-enterprise language he was part of a closely knit social organization. His conditioning made him a different type from the aggressive, often socially irresponsible small competitor who had built capitalism and industrialism in Europe and America. What the difference was to be for both business and the rest of society is a major theme of this book.

## 2

## *Fundamentals of Business Change*

Che self-made manager in business is nearing the end of his road," said an advisor on business success in 1924. "Despite his own blind faith in the 'practical' he is already hiring professionally trained engineers, chemists, accountants and hygienists . . . He must himself turn to professional education, or surrender control to those who do."[1] Exploration of what suddenly necessitated highly educated technicians and professionally trained managers after thousands of years of business by practical men inevitably leads the investigator to the technological changes taking place around the beginning of the twentieth century. Often remote from the concerns of business as such, developments in science and technology appear nevertheless to be fundamental to economic and business change. Not only do these innovating forces bring about new means of production and transportation, but the demand for capital and new ways of living and working that arise from the new machines alter the behavior of the economy and the attitudes of businessmen.

Before 1880 American life was relatively unaffected by electricity, gasoline, or fuel oil, and not at all affected by airplanes or automobiles. Late-nineteenth-century economy was characterized by the coal-burning steam engine for power, the steam locomotive for overland transportation, and heavy crude-iron and steel machinery for manufacturing. Compared to that of the twentieth century, it was a simple technology and the machines were inexpensive. The uneducated mechanic

or executive could comprehend the most complex devices and invent new ones in the course of repairing the old. The capitalist of moderate means could equip a factory. Lewis Mumford, has called this period the paleotechnic phase of industrialism.[2]
By the end of World War I a series of basic changes had occurred that presaged a new stage of business and social organization. Cheap and powerful automobiles and trucks were beginning to remold transportation and living arrangements. Electric generators, distributing power over high-voltage lines to millions of electric motors of all sizes, were displacing the steam engine. Airplanes were being mass-produced for war purposes, and would soon fly mail and passengers. For energy, gasoline and fuel oil were gaining rapidly on coal. Chemical and electrical processes together with light machinery made of alloyed metals were changing the character of factories. Three- and four-story plants with overhead shafts and belts were being replaced by lighter, cleaner one-story buildings where power moved through wires and materials flowed through pipes or rode on electrically conveyed assembly lines.

Differing forms of business organization, to be sure, may be used to administer a given stage of technology, but machinery makes certain inescapable demands. Big American corporations, for example, differed from Soviet trusts, yet since both ran the same physical type of productive units, the two types of organization had to have much in common. The large-scale complex machinery of the twentieth century could not have been owned or operated by the small business firms of 1850. A steel plant like that of Gary, Indiana, which cost some fifty million dollars in 1907, required a corresponding aggregation of capital and labor. It could not be run by a partnership with a few thousand dollars in capital. Much equipment, particularly for railroads and public utilities, was so expensive that from a financial standpoint only a monopoly of local markets could justify the investment. And in addition almost all of these large-scale processes showed lower costs per unit of product as output increased, or as the economist would say, they were operations of decreasing cost. Therefore, the bigger the company grew the greater its advantage in the market.

Up to the end of World War I, at least, advances in machinery tended to produce bigger plants and bigger business organizations, and in many cases there were no economic alternatives, although shrewd financial operators pushed bigness and monopoly to extremes not demanded by the technology itself. Nation-wide companies in which single plants frequently provided employment for a large part of the population of country towns or small cities were affected "with a public interest" no matter what their product. Hence government regulation and the "welfare state" had roots in the changes brought about by late nineteenth- and early twentieth-century technology.

Bigness and the managerial system together were the fundamental business development of the twentieth century and had their basis in technological change. The system of professional management grew up with the railroads and public utilities and moved into manufacturing late in the nineteenth century when the increasing cost of mechanized equipment began to require public sale of securities. The ultimate spread of the system to finance, trade, and service may be seen as a consequence of the demands made upon these sectors by large-scale industry and transportation.

### TECHNOLOGY, SPECIALIZATION, AND GROUP EFFORT

Save in the history of a few individual companies there has been little detailed analysis of the interaction of technological and business change, and here we can only suggest a few of the more obvious relationships. The process as a whole was one of increasing the complexity of all administrative problems. The evolving technology in the plant and more complex business controls in the office not only required care and guidance by highly educated specialists, but also group efforts at solving dilemmas that involved many factors. "In the future," wrote Frederick W. Taylor, the pioneer efficiency expert, "it will be appreciated that our leaders must be trained right as well as born right, and that no great man can [with the old system of personal management] hope to compete with a number of ordinary men who have been properly organized so as efficiently to cooperate." [3]

Factories were best staffed by college-trained men, or those who knew when and where to turn for expert advice. Mathematical problems in heat, qualities of metals, and utilization of fuel went well beyond the comprehension of the man not specially educated in these matters. The increasing use of electrochemical processes also helped to push the frontiers of progress beyond the horizon of "practical" administrator or mechanic. Commercially significant new inventions were likely to require costly application of basic scientific knowledge by group effort to machinery that had already become complicated.

Thus the source of invention and technological innovation moved from the workbench to the laboratory. And research laboratories in general were only to be found in universities, endowed foundations, large business companies, or government agencies. In big companies the pursuit of novelty was normally a group effort, directed by businesslike administrators of research. One leading chemical company came to employ 5,000 people in research activity. Thus important technological advance was not only institutionalized in the business system, but, to a degree, socialized through the research of countless scientists working for nonprofit organizations.

Although management-administered invention has been the subject of some study, it has been difficult to determine its effects. An initial problem arises in determining at what point an improvement in process becomes a new "invention." One authority has insisted that "the meaning of the conventional phrase 'mechanical invention' must be broad enough to include pure science and fine art, both of which interact continuously with mechanical invention in the narrower sense . . ." [4] Another imponderable in any effort at measurement is the relation of numbers of inventions to their importance. It seems probable that managerially directed invention leads to less patenting or immediate utilization of minor changes, but perhaps more relentless pursuit of major objectives. Regardless of the methods by which invention took place, many scholars believe that the rate of technological progress was accelerating.[5]

While some technological changes demanded new specialists, others led to new business organization to take care of higher levels of production and sales. Greater productivity frequently came from improvements in quality of materials or processes rather than increases in size of machines. Harder metals, for example, were intimately connected with increasing mass production. Harder tool steels, such as that developed by Taylor, Gantt, and White in 1900, added speed and precision to cutting machinery and allowed more processes to be mechanized. New steel played a key part in the great Ford growth. When Henry Ford saw some French vanadium steel in 1903, he is said to have exclaimed: "That is the kind of material we ought to have in our cars." [6] His executives, already familiar with the new alloy from reading British journals, used it with great effect in the famous Model T. The unprecedented sales of the Model T, in turn, led to new levels in factory size and efficiency of plant management.

Improvement in steel was continuous in the early decades of the century. Special heat treatment of older steels, such as manganese-carbon, produced better results for many purposes than vanadium or other alloys. Better furnace control of carbon and other elements made for a wider variety of steels with different qualities, and this change, in turn, led to far more complex relations between steel companies and their customers. As late as 1927 the introduction of carbide alloys made possible still harder cutting steel, an innovation that again increased precision and led to more substitution of machines for hand processes. The change represented a step forward on the long road to automation, that is, to factories with many managers and a few workers.

Machine-made, interchangeable parts were also an important factor in building big enterprises. In the early twentieth century the Cadillac automobile company gave a dramatic illustration of the increasing exactness of the machine process. The mixed parts for three cars were shipped to London and satisfactory automobiles were assembled in the presence of officials of the Royal Automobile Association. Up to the end of World War I, however, hand-finishing remained superior to machines. An automobile engine carefully fitted by expert machinists could develop as much as twice the horsepower of the same size machine-made product. But in the twenties better cutting and boring tools, adjusted by the new Johansen measuring blocks, allowed shafts and cylinders to be machined to tolerances (variations in measurement) that nearly equalled those achieved by hand-finishing. Well-fitted parts meant not only less waste of power from leakage or friction, but also more readily interchangeable parts.

Interchangeability of parts was one of the elements emphasizing the necessarily collective or coöperative character of mass production. In most lines interchangeability was of limited value to consumers until all manufacturers of the particular product joined in standardizing sizes. Reaping the harvest, therefore, was a business rather than a technological problem, and because exclusive parts favored the strong competitive position of some big firms, progress was slow. Led by its president, Harold E. Coffin, the Society of Automotive Engineers in 1910 started a campaign for intercompany technical standards. Coffin held that lack of standards was "responsible for nine-tenths of the production troubles and most of the needless expense entailed in the manufacture of motor cars." [7] For the supply companies standardization carried with it the possibility of reducing the number of styles and sizes. At first the big automobile companies were indifferent to Coffin's suggestion, but by 1925 they were participating actively, and by 1930 the battle for standardization in the industry was substantially won.

Meanwhile, Secretary of Commerce Herbert Hoover (1921–1928) had pushed the movement in other fields. Two hundred and ten different shapes of bottles were reduced to twenty; sixty-six shapes of bricks were reduced to seven; nuts, bolts, gears, and countless other common parts were similarly reduced from scores of sizes to only a few. Fewer sizes meant not only easier repairs and replacements, but also higher levels of mass production in each remaining size.

In 1900 many cutting tools had become completely automatic. This permitted one man to operate a battery of lathes or drills. In some cases 150 multiple tools could perform the same operation simultaneously under the guidance of one mechanic. The new equipment challenged managers to give thought to the reorganization of production. Frederick W. Taylor, at one time a manager, preached the value of studying the exact character of the repetitive motions made by an operator, just as a golf swing or a swimming stroke might be analyzed with a view to gaining the maximum speed and efficiency of movement. In promoting his theories at the turn of the century, he became a pioneer management consultant.

Before the introduction of fully automatic machinery, manufacturers had already discovered the advantages of a continuous process. In the case of operations carried on at high temperature, such as steelmaking, the benefit was obvious. But even where neither speed nor heat were essential, a minute division of labor and a rhythm in movement was found valuable. The big meat-packers in the 1880's had hung carcasses on trolleys and moved them along a "desembly" line where each worker detached a certain section. Electric power allowed further extension of these efficiencies in time and motion. In the first decade of the twentieth century, brewers introduced electrically run conveyors for the "assembling" of a bottle of beer. Bottles were washes, filled, capped, pasturized, labeled, and boxed in a continuous process with each worker performing a single operation or merely supervising an automatic machine. When these principles were introduced into the automobile industry by the Ford Company in 1913 and 1914, the savings in man-hours were so enormous, up to seven to one, that in popular imagination the mechanized assembly line, a managerial innovation, came to be practically synonymous with American mass production.

## TECHNOLOGY AND BUSINESS CENTERS

As an outgrowth of scientific advances and mass production there came new building materials and forms of transportation that significantly altered the invironment of business executives. It became physically possible to concentrate the head offices of the business of a nation or region into a few center-city areas. The thousands of workers who must come to the offices daily could now be brought by rapid transit from distant suburbs.

Although stone structures 150 feet high had been built since ancient times, the walls had to be so thick at the base that such buildings were not economical for apartments or offices. In the 1880's steel framework solved the masonry problem and left elevators as the chief uneconomic consumers of space. Furthermore, steel removed any foreseeable limit to height. By 1900 the downtown sections of major American cities were being rebuilt with fifteen- to twenty-five-story office buildings. Though Chicago had been the pioneer, New York was the center of early twentieth-century skyscraper construction. Fantastic things happened on Manhattan Island. In 1899 the nine-story Pabst Hotel was completed in the triangle between Broadway and Seventh Avenue at Times Square. Three years later it was torn down to make way for the new subway.[8] The Singer Sewing Machine Building, finished in 1906 as the first of the great towers, was 612 feet high, but it was surpassed time and again within the next few years until the race for height was won in 1931 by the 1,248-foot Empire State Building.[9]

The skyscraper's chief value was not in economy of construction, or even in most cases in more intensive utilization of valuable land; it was primarily a matter of advertising. It was thus a combined product of technology and the new ideas of businessmen. The building not only advertised the name of the owning company, but also gave prestige to firms renting space in it. Economically the situation was ironic; by 1900 the telephone and electric rapid-transit system made possible a decentralization of city business life, but instead the skyscraper produced greater mid-city concentration, and rapid transit was used to get thousands of employees to and from these fabulously expensive central locations.

Businessmen had barely adjusted their operations to rapid transit when the automobile began to change again the urban map. The overbuilding of the business centers, flanked by expensive hotels and apartment houses, still continued, but the automobile required new bridges, tunnels, and streets and led to the construction of thousands of suburban homes. Ultimately the automobile would produce decentralization of factories and branch offices, but up to 1930 that was still more a portent than a reality.

### THE BUSINESS CYCLE

Over and above the immediate effect of technological change on business methods and arrangements was its influence on the behavior of the system as a whole. Capital investment, productivity, and obsolescence depended upon the rate and character of technological change. The ups and downs of the business cycle, whether the nation enjoyed prosperity or suffered depression, in turn, hinged upon these same factors.

To follow this line of causation one step farther, the justification of the business system to the public rested on its ability to bring about an increasingly high standard of living, and this capacity depended on managerial discovery and use of improved technology. When, for example, in the thirties business failed to invest in new equipment at a sufficient rate, the federal government moved in on the business system. Therefore, the effect of technology on capital investment and the business cycle must be seen as fundamental to business change: as, in fact, a basic factor in the survival of a private rather than a state enterprise system.

Wesley Mitchell, the great American student of the business cycle, declared that since cumulative changes in economic organization continue to occur, each generation "will see reason to recast the theory of business cycles which they learned in their youth." [10] For this reason it is impossible in a small book, and probably fruitless in addition, to survey the varied parade of theories of the business cycle. But, thanks largely to the work of Arthur F. Burns and Wesley Mitchell, what actually happened in the way of business cycles in the twentieth century can be discussed with some accuracy.

In general, during the early part of the century, swings in the dollar volume of business, the usual measure of cyclical activity, lasted less than two years in a given direction. The social historian, however, notes a boom or depression only when one of these swings was unusually strong and ended in a strong reaction in the opposite direction. From a perspective that reveals only the high peaks or deep valleys of business activity there were general good times from 1897 to 1907, although many minor fluctuations occurred in between. Following the break in the strong upswing from 1903 to 1906 there was a relatively short depression in late 1907 and during most of 1908. From then on minor movements again characterized the cycle until a major recession that started early in 1913 was accentuated by the outbreak of war in Europe and reached a low ebb at the end of 1914. The boom touched off by Allied war orders and sustained by spending for war and reconstruction broke in the middle of 1920. The resulting depression was unprecedented in the sudden decline in volume of business, but was over by late 1922. From then on business volume went up and down about as usual, until the great financial boom of 1928 and 1929.

The effect of phases of the cycle on business opinion and on public opinion of business were obvious in the major swings. The shifts from extreme optimism to equal pessimism affected politics, family life, and even the arts. The fact that the two minor recessions between 1922 and 1929 were mild and brief colors the whole retrospective view of the 1920's and links the historical events of these years with attitudes of satisfaction and confidence.

A closer analysis would no doubt show that even the mild swings of the cycle influenced opinion both in and of business. The Progressive movement, for example, reached its height during the years 1908 to 1914 when for the nonagricultural sectors of the economy recession or depression was more the rule than prosperity. But the correlation cannot be pushed too far. Mild changes in business volume were often obscured by other public issues.

### TECHNOLOGY AND LONG-RUN CHANGE

┼Technological change underlies the business cycle insofar as it creates short-run periods of more or less rapid investment, but in the long run the cumulative rate of technological progress is registered in increases in the standard of living, popularly referred to as economic growth. It must be remembered, however, that these interactions are not automatic, the rate of investment depends in a large part on the attitudes of businessmen, and the results go far to shape the place of business in the society. It is necessary, therefore, to see changing rates of economic growth as a background for and partial explanation of what happens to business.

In a diverse society with wide differences in income, occupation, ways of life, and material desires, it is difficult to find uniform, realistic ways of measuring economic advance or stagnation. The briefest discussion of the subject becomes cluttered with special terms and clouded by ambiguous figures. Single measures of growth show only certain aspects and are obviously more accurate for tangible factors like gross national product or money income than for such intangibles as productive leisure, advance of scientific potentiality, or reserve abilities of the labor force. In measuring even the physical elements, problems arise from the uneven character of business activity. No two decades or half-decades are alike in relation to phases of the business cycle, yet any effort to introduce long-term moving averages obscures the immediate background that conditions business.

For example, suppose that real per capita income, the nearest equivalent to the sacred standard of living, is selected as a measure of progress. This term means the "national income," a widely accepted arbitrary calculation that reflects the total national production in money terms, divided by the population and adjusted for changes in price. If one takes averages for the ten-year periods 1899–1908, 1909–1918, and 1919–1928 the respective income figures are $458, $517, and $612. The standard of living appears to have advanced at an accelerating pace. If, however, one takes 1894–1903, 1909–1918, and 1924–1933, the figures are $401, $517, and $607.[11] Now the rate of growth appears to be slowing down. The difference comes from including parts of two major depressions in the terminal decades of the second series, and not in that of the first. But, whatever series are used, or whatever spans of years are selected for base periods, real per capita income advanced from 1900 to 1929 at a rate not alarmingly different from the satisfactory progress of the late nineteenth century.

Other effects of technological change on the structure of the business system and its place in society can be seen in the altered output and employment of various sectors of the economy such as manufacturing, agriculture, trade, and service. In the United States of 1800 over 90 per cent of the workers were in agriculture. The entire area of "business" was limited to 4 or 5 per cent of the population. As industrialism grew in the nineteenth century the number of workers in manufacturing rapidly increased until by 1900 some older industrial areas, such as Massachusetts, had nearly half of the working population employed in factories. But as each worker in manufacturing came to produce almost twice as much in physical goods between 1900 and 1929 the increase in this kind of employment leveled off.[12] From 1900 to 1914 the portion of the total American labor force engaged in manufacturing rose only from 21 to 22 per cent, and from 1919 to 1929 it declined very slightly. That about one-fifth to one-fourth of the labor force in manufacturing represents some plateau of maturity is indicated by the lack of radical change in the peacetime figures of 1929 and 1949.[13]

Meanwhile, the percentage of the working population engaged in agriculture continued to decline, as it had throughout the nineteenth century, and those myriad business activities classified as trade, finance, or service continued to increase.

In 1900 one American worker in three was engaged in farming; by 1929 the ratio was one in five. Trade, service, and finance occupied one worker out of four in 1900 and better than one out of three in 1929. To summarize, the three major types of activity stood in the relation of manufacturing, 3; agriculture, 5; and trade, finance, and service 3 in 1900; and respectively 3, 3, 4, in 1929.

Viewed abstractly these changes may seem slight, but when made manifest in the rise of filling stations, roadside restaurants, beauty parlors, department stores, brokerage and insurance offices — along with the reversion of unprofitable eastern farm land to forest — they symbolized a new American society, and an economy more dependent on luxury trades and less geared to crops and the weather.

In the long run the increasing standard of living is related to the investment of savings in productive equipment. Some of the investment may be unwise and the equipment useless, but in general additional equipment provides additional goods. Therefore, high rates of investment go with rapid growth, and a decline in the rate of investment results in a slackening of the rate of growth.

The efforts of individuals to save money, and of businessmen to invest it, are not always in balance. Personal saving depends largely on size of income and social habits, whereas investment depends upon the immediate promise of gains from new technology modified by business forecasts of activity in the near future (see p. 115). Thus, although estimates indicate that from 1900 to 1930 the percentage of national income being saved each year tended to increase, the portion invested in real physical equipment declined.[14] Simon Kuznets puts the percentage of national income going into net capital formation during the decade 1899–1908 at 12.6, and for 1919–1928 at 10.2.[15]

Failure to develop or use sufficient new physical equipment was directly responsible for the decline by one-fifth in the rate of net capital formation between the first and third decades of the new century, but an influence in this failure was an equal fall in the rate of increase in population. Up to 1910 the population of the continental United States had always grown more than 20 per cent each decade, and much of the new capital investment had represented the buildings and equipment needed for new families. The rate of population increase in the first decade of the twentieth century was 21 per cent, but for the second decade it was 15 per cent, and for the third 16 per cent. Had European immigration not been checked by war from 1914 to 1918, and by restrictive legislation from 1921 on, the decline in the rate might have been both less severe and more uniform. For example, from 1900 to 1914 immigrants entered the country at the rate of 890,000 a year, whereas from 1920 to 1929 the average rate was only 430,000.

Yet the change in the number of immigrants was not tremendous when seen against a background of total population. An average year of the first decade of the century produced a total increase of 1,600,000 in population, while an average year of the 1920's produced a 1,700,000 gain. The gradual decline in the rate of population increase does not seem sufficient, on the basis of present theories, to account for the sharp drop in real income that was to come in the 1930's. We must have a certain sympathy for the man of 1929 who saw no factors other than stock prices that seemed seriously out of adjustment.

The decrease in the part of the national income going into real capital formation in the 1920's, coupled with a rising rate of saving, was one reason for a money market which made it increasingly easy to sell securities. The easy money market led to real-estate and mortgage booms featured by skyscraper office buildings and hotels, to monstrous corporate holding companies tying together diverse business empires, and to extravagant hopes of the speedy elimination of poverty from the United States. On the surface there was no evidence of the lack of sufficiently great technological demand for new capital. The businessman was momentarily a hero, at the very time when he was failing to find proper uses for the people's savings. But in the end the declining trend of real capital formation toppled him from his pedestal and made him the public villain.

From the basic relations already discussed it would be possible to deduce the general characteristics of business in the first three decades of the twentieth century. But such an explanation would have to be highly generalized, and in the generalizations American business would scarcely seem different from British or German. To see business in *American* life it is necessary to examine some of the particular conditioning forces in the local environment such as the industrial pattern, political pressures, and entrepreneurial attitudes.

# Patterns of Capital and Industry

Technological change brought developments in industry and transportation that altered the environment of business. In order to understand the response of business to these physical changes, it is necessary to know some of their history. The position and attitudes of railroad management by 1930, for example, must be seen in relation to the rise of the automobile, the experience of World War I, and continuing government regulation. Similarly the growth of corporate bureaucracy, relocation and dispersal of business activity, and new problems in public relations were direct results of changes in the electrical and automobile industries. To read of business change divorced from technological or industrial history is like enjoying scenery without knowing your geographical location.

## TRENDS IN CAPITAL FORMATION

As indicated in the last chapter, the cycle of capital investment–industrial expansion–more prosperity was vitally important to the position of business in the culture. In contrast to most of the nineteenth century when capital-consuming projects took a consistently high percentage of the national income, the falling rate of capital formation after 1900 stood as a continual threat to prosperity. Except in a few years of inflationary pressure, such as those from 1916 to 1920, twentieth-century industries consuming large amounts of capital were major stabilizing elements in the economic life of the nation.

While it had always been the spirit of capitalism to make a major virtue of investment, the emphasis appears to have been accentuated during these years of increasing government regulation, higher taxes, and a declining rate of expansion. Seeing the New York stock exchanges as the central mechanism in the process of capital formation, broker Henry Clews wrote in 1900: "In the course of evolution and a higher civilization we might be able to get along comfortably without Congress, but without Wall Street never." [1] Believing that high taxes were hindering capital formation in the 1920's, Secretary of the Treasury Andrew Mellon warned: "If the sources of capital investment are dried up, the flow of all income may eventually cease." [2]

In spite of Henry Adam's belief that his generation was "mortgaged to the railroads," the chief capital-consuming activity of Americans for three hundred years had been the construction of buildings: homes, barns, sheds, stores, schools, meeting houses, mills, and factories. The construction business directly employed two and a half million workers in 1920, more than any other manufacturing activity except iron and steel, and indirectly employed a million more in factory production and transportation of building materials. For the half-decade 1925–1929 the cost of new construction averaged nearly eleven billion dollars a year.[3] A part of these totals duplicate sums counted in the capital expansion of other industries, but even so, the money going into homes was larger than the new capital invested in any general type of transportation or industry. Up to 1915 railroads remained the next largest consumers of capital, followed by the electrical industry and iron and steel. Of these, only electrical products and installations represented a change from the nineteenth-century pattern.

Aside from the development of chemicals, World War I did not do much in itself to change the pattern of American industry, but it marked a stage in the growth of electricity. Following the war the electric-utility industry — including light, power, telephone, and telegraph — became, next to building construction, the largest user of new capital. The railroads, in spite of a relative decline, continued in third place up to 1930, with capital expenditures of over eight hundred million a year. In fourth place there was a newcomer portentous of the increasing role of government in the economy: state expenditures, including federal subsidies, for public highways. And this capital outlay, exceeding a billion dollars in 1930, was growing the most rapidly. Meanwhile iron and steel, in fifth place, continued as the principal capital consumer among the purely manufacturing categories.

Though construction was the most important activity in the consumption of capital, little need be said of it from the standpoint of business development. Everything in the situation seemed to work against change. Clients were cautious and disinclined to be the guinea pigs for experiments. The construction industry was made up of thousands of small concerns whose traditional practices and specialties were written into municipal building codes. Subcontracting of the various parts of the work was the rule among small contractors, who often played the role of brokers rather than builders. Only in major cities were there big construction companies staffed by engineers alert to new technological development.

For these reasons there had been little alteration during the nineteenth century in the age-old technology of building. The steam shovel was invented in 1839, steam hoists and winches were used on steamships from the earliest days, but steam only came to the construction industry in the 1880's and 1890's. A cause of the change was the need for power machinery in handling structural steel. Steel-frame skyscrapers, and large steel bridges also brought power drills and riveters. But the later operations of building, laying the masonry and floors, placing the windows, plastering, and painting continued to be done by hand.

### THE WEB OF ELECTRICAL EQUIPMENT

The impact of electricity on public utilities, including railroads, created between 1900 and 1930 a demand for new capital investment second only to that of housing. The telephone spread rapidly, particularly after the expiration of Bell's basic patents in 1894, and by 1930 this form of communication, nationally organized by the American Telephone & Telegraph Company, had a capital investment of over four billion dollars.

Still more had been put into street and suburban electric railways. Frank J. Sprague had opened the way for this investment when he demonstrated the success of the overhead power wire and trolley in Richmond, Virginia, in 1887. Trolleys reached their height at the time of World War I when 1280 companies operated 40,000 miles of track capitalized at $5,000,-000,000. With sufficient patience one could travel from New York to Boston by trolley. The downtown sections of cities were a maze of trolley lines.

In addition to the spread of rapid transit, the steam railroads spent hundreds of millions of dollars on the electrification of entrances to major cities, and of a few long-distance lines.

During these thirty years an investment as big as that of the nineteenth century in railroads was made in urban power and light stations. Generally built by local interests, but often controlled by big holding companies, these stations by 1930 had a value of some ten billion dollars. In the nineties progressive entrepreneurs were introducing electrical equipment into industry, in 1895 dynamos were built for a great hydroelectric station at Niagara Falls, and by 1905 it could be said that practically all factories and shops in the United States of any size, constructed in the new century, used an electric drive either exclusively or for most purposes.

Reshaping industrial processes by the dynamo led to new business problems and opportunities. Unlike steam power, which was efficiently produced only by big engines close by their furnaces and boilers, electric power was almost infinitely divisible and could travel hundreds of miles. The current from remote central generators could run small electric motors hitched to each individual tool or machine. Factories no longer needed to be mazes of shafts and driving belts.

Cheap electric power and cheap labor led northern companies to build textile mills in the South. In contrast to the three or four stories most economical for steam power, one-story buildings, located in country towns, could be operated by electricity with women and girls hired from the surrounding area. Since the head office of the textile firms usually remained in the North, management had to learn how to operate plants, with untrained labor, a thousand miles away.

Compared to the sums invested in connection with electrical installations, the capital in electrical manufacturing and the annual value of the product were small before World War I.[4] The new equipment was developed chiefly by two firms: General Electric, formed by a merger of the Edison and the Thomson-Houston Electric companies in 1892; and the older Westinghouse Electric Company. These concerns signed an agreement in 1897 to share their patents, and succeeded thereafter in preventing the rise of general competitors in the field of lighting and heavy equipment.

### THE OLDER FORMS OF TRANSPORTATION

The massive mechanical achievement of nineteenth-century Americans had been in railroad transportation. By 1900 travelers and goods went by rail. Trunk and branch lines crisscrossed the entire country. Except in the mountain West most farmers were no more than ten miles from a station. Only a few worn descendants of the proud river steamers of an earlier day still ran, and only a few slow-moving, bulky products were transported by river or canal barge.

This railroad supremacy in long-haul transportation was first menaced in 1914, not by the motor truck, which before the general use of pneumatic tires about 1920 was not a serious competitor, but by the completion of the Panama Canal. The Canal had been started in 1904, but epidemics of malaria and yellow fever and then landslides in the deep cuts delayed the work. In the face of its impending completion, however, three additional transcontinental rail connections had been pushed through. By 1905 the San Pedro, Los Angeles, and Salt Lake City line connected the cities named in its title as parts of the Union Pacific System. In 1909 the Chicago, Milwaukee, and St. Paul completed an electrified extension from Aberdeen, South Dakota, to Seattle, Washington; and in 1911 the Gould interests finished the Western Pacific from Salt Lake City to San Francisco. Eventually the needs of World War II and the rapid growth of the West Coast justified these additional roads through the mountains, but the opening of the Canal in 1914 temporarily put them in a poor competitive position. Furthermore, the large quantity of ship tonnage built by the government as an emergency measure during and immediately after World War I reduced the price of ships to less than $10 a dead-weight ton and stimulated water competition. Even with relatively high canal tolls, slow-moving freighters could draw cargo from hundreds of miles inland and still undercut the coast-to-coast railroad rates.

In the long run the rise in the cost of constructing ships and in the wages of stevedores was to minimize competition by water. The really dangerous competitor to the railroad became the truck, which during the twenties cut deeply into the railroad business. The combined effect of competition by road and water is shown by the fact that while the railroads in 1929 carried only 50 per cent more ton miles of freight than in 1913, the best year prior to the outbreak of World War I, the physical volume of manufacturing over the same period had increased 80 per cent.

In miles of track the year 1930 marked the peak of railroad growth. Railroad routes, mostly single-track, had lengthened by a third from 1900 to 1915 and then remained fairly constant at about 260,000 miles from 1916 to 1932. Up to 1930 additional sidings, and double and quadruple tracks had been put down every year. This total grew by 25 per cent between 1900 and World War I, and then about 10 per cent more by 1930.

Automobiles, robbing branch lines of their passengers, started a descending spiral; fewer passengers meant fewer trains; and fewer trains led erstwhile passengers to go by car instead. At the same time trucks were gradually stealing the freight business. Each year the roads petitioned state and federal commissions to allow the abandonment of certain branch-line services. With the coming of depression new construction no longer compensated for abandonment. The year ending June 31, 1931, was the first one in American history in which there was a decrease in miles of railroad track.

In meeting the challenge of growing competition, the railroad companies were in a different position from other American business. Through the Hepburn Act of 1906 the Interstate Commerce Commission had been given effective power to regulate rates and to prevent railroads from entering into other types of activity. Subsequent acts of 1910 and 1913 extended the powers of the Commission to cover railroad finance, accounting, and changes in rates. During these years the Interstate Commerce Commission viewed its function more as that of a policeman curbing bad actions by the roads than as an authority planning for their ultimate welfare. From January 1918 to March 1920, the needs of war forced the government to run the railroads under a series of lease agreements. Whether or not the roads received what they deserved under these contracts, they at least failed to make the large wartime profits that accrued to many other businesses. The roads faced their first decade of keen competition from other carriers with no large accumulated surplus to finance improvements.

One of the least expensive ways of improving railroad efficiency was consolidation of competing or connecting lines. This could prevent much duplication of service and equipment. The Transportation Act of 1920, which codified the existing regulations and made certain new additions, authorized the Interstate Commerce Commission to work out plans for consolidation. Any railroad-initiated consolidations had to be approved by the Commission. This produced a virtual impasse. The Commission's plans were for the stronger roads to consolidate with the weaker ones to form evenly balanced systems. The private plans were for the consolidation of the stronger roads only, with the weaker ones left out in the cold. As a result few important consolidations took place.

Other lines of approach to lower costs were through the installation of labor-saving equipment and more efficient operation. But efforts at greater efficiency were often met by opposition from the Brotherhood Unions, some of whose members would be deprived of jobs or forced to work harder. Perhaps a more vigorous and imaginative group of managers would have found ways to make sweeping changes in spite of these obstacles, possibly a generation of strict government and banker control (see p. 86) had sapped the initiative of railroad executives, but in any case, change took the form of gradual improvement in existing types of equipment and ways of doing things.

Nevertheless, the sum of these minor advances was far from negligible. Secretary of Commerce Herbert Hoover said in his *Annual Report* for 1927 that the improvement in railroad service was "probably the most outstanding industrial accomplishment since the war." [5] Steam engines became more efficient, longer trains (both freight and passenger) became the rule, and the hauling of empty cars was greatly reduced. In 1929, 20 per cent fewer employees produced about the same operating revenue at about the same freight and passenger rates as in 1920.

THE AUTOMOTIVE REVOLUTION: FIRST PHASE

The improvement in railroad efficiency seemed sufficient in the years of prosperity and might have continued so against less rapidly evolving competitors than the young automobile companies. While the railroad by World War I had reached the stage of maturity where change would probably be slow in any case, the automobile was in its youth, and the truck and bus in their infancy.

The automobile business, from the standpoint of plant and equipment, including highways, materials of production, and the effect of its needs and products on other businesses was part of an emerging twentieth-century industrial complex. Into this new group, whose ownership and products interlocked in such companies as Du Pont and General Motors, may be placed automotive and airplane parts, light electrical machinery including household equipment, synthetic chemicals, and older products that came to be chiefly associated with the automobile such as glass, rubber, and special types of metals. Although the obvious emphasis in this group was on durable and semidurable goods used directly by consumers, these companies also developed new materials, machines, and processes that entered into other types of manufacturing. The development of quick-drying lacquers for use on automobiles, for example, radically altered the production and use of paint and varnish.

The automobile had its origins in France and Germany. Comparison of the French Panhard-Levassor of 1895 with the attempts of American mechanics to build horseless carriages in this same year reveals a striking example of poor technical and business communication across national boundaries. The few men who read technical journals in French and German were not interested in this apparently useless toy of wealthy playboys, and the practical American mechanics who experimented with automobiles did not read foreign-language magazines. Some other factors, however, help to explain the primitive character of the American designs.

Many of the early American automotive entrepreneurs were men familiar with the large bicycle companies that flourished in the eighties and nineties. American rural roads were of dirt or gravel that would not support a long, heavy vehicle in bad weather. Both manufacturers and potential customers thought in terms of bicycle and carriage design. Consequently, the Haynes, Duryeas, Appersons, and Popes of the middle nineties designed buggies with bicycle-type wheels that would have a high clearance and be light enough to be pushed out of trouble. Such a car did not need the four-cylinder motor, three-speed transmission, and heavy steel frame of the French cars. A single cylinder under the high seat of a wooden buggy seemed enough to provide all the speed that the roads would permit.

Commercial manufacture of such "horseless carriages" started in 1894, and in 1899, the first year of large production, some 4,000 cars were manufactured by fifty-seven supply and assembly shops. The number of firms involved illustrates a characteristic of automobile production that lasted for several decades: the company that ultimately placed its trademark on the car was only the final assembler of parts made by a number of specialists. Rubber companies supplied tires, bicycle-makers wheels and other parts, wagon builders the bodies, and some of the numerous American machine shops began to specialize in motors. Since most of these firms, well established in their other lines of business, would supply the parts on credit, the automobile assembler needed only a large empty building, some simple tools and machines, and a few workers. Entry into the business required little capital. Ford, for example, started in 1903 with paid-in funds of only $28,500.

On the production side the automobile used suppliers that were already highly developed; on the consumption side no other nation presented a potential demand equal to that of the United States. The size of the country and its scattered population had always made better transportation a major interest. Doctors, lawyers, salesmen, executives, policemen, firemen, and farmers all needed to get around faster. Good profits for both businessmen and farmers in the years after 1896, as well as generally high middle-class salary levels, gave millions of Americans the ability to speed up their lives with this new thousand-dollar utility.

Although manufacture started on a small scale in both the East and the Middle West, within a decade there was the beginning of concentration in southeastern Michigan. Here there were the necessary subsidiary industries, a good labor supply, transportation, and perhaps most important of all, bankers willing to extend credit. The earliest companies to win a nation-wide market, such as Oldsmobile, Cadillac, and Packard, were located there.

In the beginning it was not certain that the gasoline automobile would become the standard type. A number of makers of steam engines put out steamers that had advantages in speed, flexibility, and ease of driving. But they were heavier than gasoline cars with equal horsepower, could not be started until steam was raised in the boiler, and if carelessly handled could explode. The electric car, powered by a storage battery, was easier to operate, but heavier in relation to its power and slower moving than its rivals. The latter handicap was gradually reduced, but the need for recharging the battery about as often as a gas tank would have had to be filled was ultimately fatal to the popularity of the electric.

The Electric Motor Vehicle Company, financed by New York and Philadelphia traction magnates, was not only in a position to push electric cars, but also held an American patent on the internal combustion engine. These big operators, however, did not choose to invest the sums necessary to improve storage batteries and eliminate delays from recharging by establishing battery-exchange stations throughout the country. Since the Electric Company's patent was a weak one, and it was not prepared to monopolize the field, it licensed gasoline-car producers on a very low royalty basis until Henry Ford won a court decision in 1911 that held the patent nonapplicable to the type of cars being manufactured. By World War I production of both steam and electric passenger cars had come to an end.

With some companies producing nearly 10,000 cars a year in 1908, mass production, judged by then current standards, had been achieved. At this point William C. Durant of the Buick Company sought to gain a more secure position in the market by widespread consolidation, and Henry Ford planned to improve the sales of his company by concentrating on a simpler and better product at a relatively low price. Both plans mirrored the background of their proponents: Durant was an experienced executive and promoter from the wagon business, Ford an "engineer" from electrical and machinery companies. According to their own fashion, both plans worked. Without substantial Wall Street aid Durant combined seventeen companies into General Motors with stock of a par value of $12,500,000. Included were Buick, Cadillac, Oldsmobile, and Oakland, which had prospered in different medium-to-high price fields, as well as a number of parts manufacturers and less successful makes of cars that were soon discontinued. Meanwhile, Henry Ford, declining a noncash offer to sell out to Durant, planned his famous Model T.

In the beginning the Model T was no cheaper than its competitors, but it was built to stand rough use over country roads, and to be repaired by country mechanics. In 1909, the first year of production, it did not lead the industry in sales. Though the assembly process for the new car was carefully planned, it was not radically different from that used by other large companies. It was the popularity and reliability of the Model T over several years that raised sales to a level where price reductions and new plant efficiencies were possible.

In fact, economies in production time were literally forced by the enormous increases in orders. By 1910 the Ford was the largest selling car, and in 1914 of the 560,000 cars sold in the United States, 250,000 were Fords. Reinvesting his profits in expanded production facilities, Ford was able to bring the price of the car below $500, and this, in turn, built further sales.

The most significant changes in Ford production came in 1913 and 1914. Instead of assembling major parts of the car at various "stations," which meant bringing the unassembled parts to certain points and then carrying the assembled subsections somewhere else, the developing car was routed on a conveyor belt past a continuous line of parts and workers. These parts in turn came from subassembly lines. This arrangement permitted minute division of labor, careful routing of all parts, a controlled speed of operation, and automatic removal of finished products. It cut the time of assembling a Ford by nearly 90 per cent. The whole process rested heavily on electrification and precision machinery that permitted complete interchangeability of parts.

Although these innovations in procedure, thought out by C. W. Avery and William Klarin in consultation with Ford, were revolutionary in their significance, they rested on the application of known and tested principles to a complex process. This new development in American mass production was an innovation in management, a better ordering or "rationalization" of operations, rather than an advance in technology.

Meanwhile other companies had grown rapidly by manufacturing high- and medium-priced cars. The growth of large-scale parts makers, like Continental Motors, which could supply all the materials necessary for a car at wholesale prices reflecting the economies of mass production, permitted nearly a hundred small-scale assemblers like Louis Chevrolet to market under their own names. These small shops, turning out a few thousand cars a year, were still scattered all over the East and Middle West, but the larger operators were concentrated in Michigan, in or near Detroit. While General Motors, into which the Du Ponts and their Chevrolet Company came in 1917, was selling an increasing share of the medium-priced cars, the day of drastic competitive pressure on the smaller companies had not yet arrived.[6]

Many things, however, worked continuously against the small company. Although it could turn out its product at a cost that allowed it to compete in the medium-priced range with the biggest companies, it was at a disadvantage in marketing. The larger company could support many more dealers, who not only sold more cars but assured convenient repair service. The big company could also afford larger advertising budgets. Even in 1912, half the cars were produced by seven companies. By 1923, 90 per cent originated in ten companies. By the end of World War I investment bankers reconciled themselves to the continued existence of this "luxury" business and were financing the larger companies, except Ford. The latter wanted no Wall Street influence in his operations, and kept virtually complete ownership in his own family.

In the mid-twenties a group of production men and New York financiers organized a rival to Ford and General Motors. This last major entrant into the passenger car industry was built around the executive ability of Walter P. Chrysler, formerly of General Motors. He reorganized the waning Maxwell Company, designed a new line of cars bearing his own name, and then merged with Dodge Brothers, one of the largest producers of moderately low-priced cars. From this time on, in good years and in bad, Chrysler, Ford, and General Motors continued to sell over 80 per cent of the passenger vehicles made in America.

The 1920's not only rounded out the automotive industrial complex, but established the car as a basic necessity. The old open touring car was a fair-weather vehicle, used largely for pleasure and often jacked up in the winter. The closed car, which rapidly became the rule in the mid-twenties, represented the trend to year-round utilitarian operation and thus not only consumed enormous quantities of plate glass and cloth upholstery, but also required millions of gallons of alcohol or glycerine for winter driving.[7]

From 1918 to 1923 the automobile business had been a major consumer of new capital, but like the trend to closed cars, other changes in the business during the middle twenties were more closely associated with marketing than with major innovations requiring heavy capital investment. Sales were stimulated by the spread of installment buying, long used for goods like furniture and pianos. By 1925 nearly three billion dollars' worth of new and used cars and trucks, some 60 per cent of the total, were sold on time.[8] Together with radios, refrigerators, and vacuum cleaners, automobile installments made "finance company" a household word. The requirement that financed cars be insured also gave an enormous boost to automobile insurance.

As the used-car market grew and old automobiles became more reliable, people with smaller incomes could afford to buy. Now the manufacturer of a new car was not only in competition with other new cars in his own price range, but with second-hand cars of all ages and sizes. This also made it easier for those in the higher income groups to trade their old cars for new ones more frequently, and it put a premium on superficial changes in style.

Style changes, cheap second-hand cars, and installment buying all hurt the sales of the Ford Model T. Even though its price was well under that of its chief competitors in the new-car field, many customers preferred to buy a bigger second-hand car for the same price or, by resort to financing, to pay more for a fancier new car. Furthermore Henry Ford refused to make concessions to changes in style and taste. In 1922 his dealers pled with him for more glamor in the Model T. He is reported to have listened without interest and replied: "Well, gentlemen, so far as I can see the only trouble with the Ford car is — that we can't make them fast enough." [9] Meanwhile his chief competitors, such as General Motors, Dodge, and Chrysler, increased the range of colors, upholsteries, and models available in their cheapest cars. When the falling sales of Model T finally forced Henry Ford to act, he was quite unprepared to bring out a new car. Production of the Model T was ended in 1927, and it took a year with no production to prepare for the Model A. Ford's abandonment of the Model T ended efforts by the largest manufacturers to sell a small cheap car.

During the next twenty-five years "small" cars grew larger and, from the mid-thirties on, more expensive. This may well represent a normal trend in the companies making complicated durable goods. Rather than reflect manufacturing economies in price cuts, which always threaten competitive warfare, lower costs are absorbed by bigger and more elaborate models.

The motor truck and bus started reorganizing the social and economic life of the nation in the twenties without attracting much attention from the pundits of the day. Two volumes prepared in 1928 by the National Bureau of Economic Research on *Recent Economic Changes* do not include either bus or truck in the index and have no discussion of automotive transportation. The freight that trucks took away from the railroads, at this time, was chiefly for short hauls of less than carload lots, and railroadmen regarded such business as generally unprofitable. Not until depression struck in the thirties were railroad economists seriously alarmed.

Trucks first reached 10 per cent of passenger-car registration in 1918. Between then and 1930 the number in operation increased nearly sixfold to a total of three and a half million. More than 75 per cent of these were in the service of the owner, and most of them were under two tons. Common and contract carrying in large trailer trucks was only beginning to be important by the end of the twenties.

As trucks became commercially important, the leading passenger-car companies either bought specialized truck builders, as General Motors did the Yellow, or, as Ford did, started plants of their own. In the case of Autocar and Reo the truck lines remained after the companies gave up passenger-car production.

Buses produced by the same companies developed more slowly than trucks. In 1925 there were only 18,000 registered, and of the 41,000 in use by 1930 probably more than half were school buses. This last fact underlines the profound social significance of motor vehicles. One of the greatest advances in education, the replacement of the one-room school with a single harassed teacher and short periods of instruction by the consolidated township school was a direct result of the bus.

Much of the capital investment associated with the rise of automotive transportation was indirect. In addition to highways, bridges, service stations, and new shops, automobiles and trucks were the chief cause of massive investments in the production of oil, rubber, and lacquers. The great upsurge in motors from 1914 to 1929 was reflected in the growing size of these auxiliary industries. The shift to closed cars in the mid-twenties made the automobile the largest consumer of glass and led to new products such as safety glass. The automobile had become one of the chief users of steel. The development in 1927 of the continuous steel rolling mill, involving the costliest plant investments up to that time, and the development of cold rolling in the 1930's were in large part responses to the demand of automobiles for thin uniform sheet metal.

By 1930 the effects of the automobile were noticeable in social habits and attitudes. The automobile companies and their leaders became the best known companies and businessmen. The cost and newness of the family's car began to replace the house as the most universally recognized mark of economic prestige, and like the armorial trappings of the medieval knight the car could always be in evidence. The small village store off the main highway which could not offer the variety of goods now available in a larger town a few minutes away disappeared. In cities there was a tendency for new shopping centers to develop along highways that by-passed the old business district. The suburbs grew, and even villages lost people to the surrounding country. Commuters came to depend upon the automobile as a means of getting to work, and cities like Detroit and Los Angeles that first became large in the age of the automobile used highways rather than elevateds or subways. The gasoline shortage of World War II was to demonstrate painfully that the automobile was a central element in American life.

No one has or perhaps can reliably estimate the vast size of capital invested in reshaping society to fit the automobile. Such a figure would have to include expenditures for consolidated schools, suburban and country homes, and changes in business location, as well as the more direct investments mentioned above. This total capital investment was probably the major factor in the boom of the 1920's, and hence in the glorification of American business.

The social and economic effect of the airplane was far slower than that of the automobile. Up to 1930 neither airplane manufacture nor commercial air transport had achieved importance as areas for capital investment, or had affected methods of business. The mention of planes in this period is made here because of their subsequent growth. From the Wright Brothers' demonstration of heavier-than-air flight at Kitty Hawk in 1903 to World War I planes were in an experimental stage. European nations, already more advanced in the construction of airplanes, developed them greatly in World War I. In America a number of leaders of the automobile business invested in plane factories to meet the war demand. Parts makers for automobiles added airplane parts and motors.

But neither the United States government nor the traveling public showed much interest in commercial aviation. Up to 1925 the federal government did little to develop airmail and nothing to establish passenger routes. The Kelly Act of 1925 marked the beginning of systematic subsidies. In addition, the government supplied beacons and weather service, and municipalities built airports essential for pioneer routes. With fourteen companies under contract for flying mail by 1926, commercial transport was underway.

But passenger travel was negligible. Accidents were frequent enough to make planes appear dangerous, and fares were higher than first-class rail rates. The air transport industry received its best publicity from successful private flights. In 1927 Charles A. Lindbergh flew to Paris alone in an ordinary single-motor plane. During the same year Richard E. Byrd, Bernt Balchen, and others made spectacular polar flights. These were followed by a brief buying wave for private planes, and a slight increase in commercial passengers. Ironically, the great American distances which had caused the railroad to spread more rapidly than in any European country seemed to operate against air passenger travel. Air travel in Europe simplified the crossing of international boundaries and was generally accomplished by short flights over lowlands on routes with many alternate landing places. In the United States there was no need to avoid customs inspection, and major trips often involved relatively long flights over dangerous territory such as the Appalachian or Rocky Mountains.

### NEW CAPITAL FOR IRON AND STEEL

The remaining major consumer of capital during the first decades of the twentieth century was the old and well-established iron and steel industry. During the years after the turn of the century, capital was used to shift from the Bessemer process, which had originated large-scale steel manufacture in Great Britain in the 1860's, to the open-hearth method. Lake Superior ores, which had come to make up three-quarters of the American supply, were particularly well suited to open-hearth smelting. Such furnaces could also utilize scrap of all kinds, as well as a wide range of ores. This process was almost as old as the Bessemer, but the need for more exact temperature control and better furnaces had held back its use until the 1890's. Increasing rapidly each year, it surpassed the Bessemer process in 1900 and by 1914 was responsible for nearly 75 per cent of the output.

Adjustment to Superior ore carried southward in specially designed ships, moved steel plants to cities near the Great Lakes. In the first decade of the twentieth century Lackawanna Steel, for example, moved from Scranton to Buffalo, and United States Steel built a gigantic plant at Gary, Indiana. Cuban and Chilean ore, however, kept other companies, such as Pennsylvania and Bethlehem, in the East. The rise of a demand for special quality steels, which had made up about 10 per cent of the total in 1900 and constituted 50 per cent by 1914, not only kept small eastern mills operating, but added to their number. The automobile industry, ultimately steel's best nonmilitary customer, also required special grades. As noted above, the need for thin uniform sheets for automobile bodies led to the continuous strip rolling mill, the greatest capital-consuming innovation of the twenties.

United States Steel, formed in 1901 by a merger of big companies, such as Carnegie and Federal, controlled 45 per cent of the ingot capacity in its early years. World War I built up Bethlehem, and a new management after 1928 expanded Republic. By 1930 these three companies had 60 per cent of the productive capacity, but United States Steel's individual share was less than before the war. During the next generation, in spite of depression, wars, and a record-breaking prosperity, the share of the market held by the dozen leading steel companies did not greatly change.[10]

CHEMICALS BECOME IMPORTANT

Far less important in its immediate effect on either business structure or capital investment than automobiles, electricity, or steel, the chemical industry nevertheless joined them in bringing great changes in methods and products. The industry had several nearly separate divisions. Manufacture of pharmaceuticals such as medicines and toilet preparations was old in 1900 and in the hands of many companies whose operations were relatively small-scale. The "heavy chemicals" division concerned with the extraction and refining of natural products like potash, carbon, and sulphur, or the preparation of simple inorganic compounds such as acids, alkalies, and carbides, also had a long history in America. Increasing about threefold between 1900 and 1914, these operations conducted by moderately large companies became a major industrial group. But most interesting from the standpoint of social change were the rise of new synthetic processes for such varied products as dyes, fibers, and plastics, and the wider use of chemical knowledge by businessmen.

World War I gave many opportunities to the well-established chemical companies. Military demands for powder and heavy chemicals greatly increased both production and profits. Companies like Du Pont accumulated surplus funds that could be invested in new ventures. A major opportunity came from the confiscation of German chemical patents by the federal government and their sale to American producers. Formulas for dyes were the most immediately important of these foreign processes, and American companies at once attempted their manufacture. In 1922 the government aided the new industry by a high tariff on dyes. But as a Du Pont official wrote a generation later, this country was a "Science Sahara." "The job called for a brand of expert technology that existed nowhere in America." [11] Although ultimately successful, the company claimed to have sunk $43,000,000 in dyes before making a profit.[12]

During the years between about 1915 and 1925, the chemical industry acquired its modern structure with four or five big firms doing a third or more of the total volume of business. Recognizing the rapidity of change, these companies safeguarded themselves by making a wide variety of products and supporting a large amount of research. From such efforts in the twenties came the commercial production of rayon, new plastics, lacquers, enamels, and dyes, while research was carried on that would result in new products such as nylon a dozen years later.

As chemical knowledge spread it revised procedures in other types of business. Oil, steel, glass, and rubber production, cloth and furniture manufacture, are just a few of the activities affected by new chemical processes. So wide was the spread that the limits of the chemical industry became indistinct. Rayon, for example, was considered by the census bureau as a part of chemical production, while oil refining was part of a separate petroleum industry. Business executives did not have to be chemists, but in most big operations they needed chemical advice.

PERMANENCE AND CHANGE

Alongside the areas of industry that were giving a lift to the economy through rapid growth in both products and fixed capital were the old, relatively mature businesses that still employed the bulk of the labor and occupied the time of the largest group of industrial businessmen. Ranking right behind construction, iron and steel, and machinery in employment of workers were three of the first industries to use power machinery: prepared foods, lumber, and textiles. Flour mills surpassed all other uses of water power in the eighteenth century, sawmills early put the steam engine to use, and textiles ushered in the modern factory.

In spite of its age the textile business, as already noted, underwent important changes between 1900 and 1930. In addition to changes brought by electricity and relocation, ring spinning and the Northrup loom for weaving increased the productivity of cotton machinery and lessened the need for skilled labor. Southern interests promoted movement to their section. When the Pepperell Company was ready to build a mill at Opelika, Alabama, in 1925, "a group of citizens were willing . . . to convey enough land for a mill and its village and to give other inducements. In fact, they gave over 300 acres, as well as $62,500 in cash, and promised no taxes for five years and a low assessment thereafter." [13] Spurred by such inducements textile plants continued to move southward decade after decade. In 1890, 76 per cent of the nation's cotton spindles were in New England; by 1930 only about 40 per cent remained there. In general, the cheapest materials were being made in the cotton-producing states, while the finer goods still came from the North.

There were also marked changes in textile consumption. The yardage of women's clothes shrank by one-half, and rayon and silk displaced cotton and wool for men's and women's underwear, socks, dresses, and suits. Offsetting this decline was a great increase in the use of cotton for tire cords and wool for automobile upholstery.

Because the early lumber business consumed its timber resources with no regard for the future, its shift in location between 1900 and 1910 was even more dramatic than in the case of cotton. In 1899, 70 per cent of the timber came from the Great Lakes and Northern Appalachian regions; in 1909, the greatest year of United States lumber output, nearly 60 per cent came from the South and about half of the remainder came from the Pacific Coast. Meanwhile, large firms like the Weyerhaeuser Timber Company, foreseeing the danger of ultimate exhaustion of resources, planned production in relation to the growing cycle of the trees that were cut. As a result some stability was produced in the new location of operations.

Prepared food, the most important of this trio of original industries, also moved and changed, but less than the other two. Factory-baked breads, packaged cereals, and canned goods gained popularity, particularly among the increasing number of city dwellers. Canning became a major business on the Pacific Coast. Railroad refrigerator cars allowed packers to move nearer the cattle of the South and West, to such cities as Fort Worth and Omaha; changes in railroad rates and storage practices brought the flour-milling center back from Minneapolis to Buffalo.

While electricity and many special situations led to new factory location and design, automotive transportation, which was to be the strongest force for change in location, had only begun its effect by 1930. The area east of the Mississippi and north of Ohio and the Mason-Dixon Line had lost only a little of its concentration of manufacturing, and its factories and business offices clustered tightly around the major railroad centers.

The last years of the 1920's which seemed so dynamic to businessmen of the time were actually the beginning of a period of stagnation. Only buildings and roads consumed capital at increasing rates. In a recent study, dividing manufacturing into fourteen major industries and one miscellaneous category, the rate of capital change is seen to turn downward in every series after 1925.[14] Businessmen were failing to find enough attractive areas for investment beyond the sterile circle of stock speculation, or the erection of larger office buildings.

The failure of business to expand sufficiently rapidly to insure full employment between 1925 and 1940 was no doubt the result of many factors. The increasing productivity of capital equipment was one of these.[15] Another may have been that a sort of technological plateau had been reached where no major innovation invited great new capital investment. Still another reason, mentioned earlier, was a leveling off of population increase. At all events, businessmen of 1929, exhilarated by the great industrial progress of the twentieth century, were generally unaware of the impending crisis.

# 4

## The Implication of Big Business

The rise of the large business corporation in the late nineteenth and twentieth centuries is one of the major changes in history, comparable to the rise of medieval feudalism or of commercial institutions at the close of the middle ages. Relatively unrestricted by political controls or traditions, the modern business corporations grew and multiplied prodigiously in the favorable climate of the United States. Corporate enterprise gradually altered the meaning of property, the circumstances and motivations of economic activity, and the careers and expectations of most citizens.

### THE BASIS OF BIGNESS

One basis for precocious growth in the size of corporate business units was the scale of machinery suitable for processing cheap and abundant natural resources for the world's largest home market. American technology might occasionally lag from the standpoint of scientific efficiency, but it usually led the world in scale of operations. The steady increase in the most efficient size for furnaces, rolling mills, multiple drills and presses, and other automatic machinery eliminated the small plant from many lines of activity.

But bigness in a single plant had its limits. Beyond a certain size, varying for different industries, two or more plants became preferable to one. William Knudsen, the famous automotive engineer, for example, disagreed with Henry Ford

51

over the latter's insistence on concentrating all his operations at the River Rouge plant near Detroit. "If we are going to move everything down there," Knudsen contended, "some day you will have 100,000 people working there." "That's what I expect," replied Ford. "I think that is too many people working in one place," Knudsen argued, "I think we have too many people here at Highland Park. I think we ought to spread out more. I think the ideal manufacturing unit consists of anywhere from 5,000 to 10,000 people . . . " [1]

As we have noted, advances in technology also made it increasingly easy for companies to spread out. Communication, the nervous system of business, was improved by the teletype, telephoto, microfilm, automobile, and airplane. Mechanized office equipment multiplied records, and punch cards and filing systems facilitated their use. Such devices, together with advances in accounting techniques, allowed management to maintain a head office in a metropolitan center, close to chief market and financial connections, and from there to exercise efficient supervision over plants located in lower-cost areas or closer to raw materials. More exact scientific controls over materials and processes lessened the risk from variable quality in multiplant operations. Exactly the same product, even one as delicate as beer, could be manufactured in plants three thousand miles apart. By mid-century companies might have fifty to a hundred plants located throughout the country. As a result, although corporations and their managements grew larger, individual plants were usually kept at the size best suited to their particular operations.

Technological change was only one of the factors leading to bigger business organizations. A commanding position in the market was often the major incentive.[2] Market considerations seemed to favor the big company. Since smaller rivals would not want to risk a price battle with a giant, the big company alone or with a few competitors could set the price of its products. Larger volume reduced the cost per unit of advertising, public relations, research, and many other incidental costs.

Before 1880 large corporations with thousands of employees and stockholders were chiefly confined to railroads and public utilities. The pressures of competition and the possibility of exploiting an increasingly great national market led to a series of corporate mergers in the eighties and nineties that resulted in clusters of big firms in many areas of economic activity. In the business upswing that began in 1897, following Bryan's defeat by McKinley, the birth rate of corporate giants became so high as to raise doubts among forward-looking intellectuals regarding the continuance of the competitive or free-enterprise system. Yet the people of the country, whether businessmen, professionals, workers, or farmers, were undoubtedly in favor of small, competitive enterprise. Consequently battle was joined between the people's representatives and the "trusts," with the former somewhat hampered by the paradox of demanding regulation in the name of free enterprise.

In the late eighties the states of Ohio and New York started suits against the trust form of corporate mergers. This was a device initiated by the Standard Oil Company in 1879, whereby the stockholders of a number of corporations turned their stock and its voting rights over to a group of trustees, who then acted as the directors of the merged firms. The New York State Court of Appeals held in the North River Sugar Refining Case in 1890 "that the effect of the defendant's action was to divest itself of the essential and vital elements of its franchise by placing them in trust . . . But graver still . . . It has helped create an anomalous trust which is, in substance and effect, a partnership of twenty corporations . . . It is a violation of the law for corporations to enter into partnership." [3] The Ohio Supreme Court went further in the Standard Oil case and held that the object of the trust "was to establish a virtual monopoly . . . Throughout the entire country . . . All such associations are contrary to the policy of our state and void." [4]

Meanwhile, the Republican members of Congress, in return for Western support of the protective tariff, had passed a strongly worded antitrust law. The Sherman Act of 1890 prohibited "every contract, combination in the form of trust or otherwise, or conspiracy, in restraint of trade or commerce among the several states." This strong and sweeping federal language, in conjunction with the attitude of the state courts, might seem to have imposed barriers to mergers or monopolistic corporations.

But this did not prove to be the case. "The trusts wriggled out of the court's grasp." [5] Even before the New York and Ohio courts rendered their decisions against the trustee device, New Jersey had made the trust unnecessary by passing a general incorporation act for holding companies. This New Jersey Act of 1889, legalizing what had been universally prohibited in general incorporation acts, hindered state antitrust prosecutions. By 1904 the seven biggest industrial companies had New Jersey charters. Meanwhile the United States Supreme Court seemed loathe to apply the Sherman Act against big unified manufacturing companies. In 1895 the justices ruled that a monopoly of manufacture was not directly a restraint of trade.[6] "The effect of this decision," wrote Theodore Roosevelt, "was . . . the absolute nullification of the anti-trust law." [7] On the other hand the Court ruled in 1899 that a contract between medium-sized companies governing conditions of interstate sales was a violation of the antitrust law.[8]

The lesson seemed fairly clear. Merger through a holding company was permissible because it involved no contracts or agreements between competitors. The Standard Oil Company adopted this form. Buying up of rivals and merging them into one big company was also legal, at least in manufacturing. But efforts by small companies to control markets by cartels or agreements were illegal. Because of these judicial interpretations the Sherman Act has been referred to as the "mother of trusts."

### BIG BUSINESS AND PROGRESSIVISM

In the period from the turn of the century to World War I both big and small business became involved with different aspects of the varied but rather steady pressures for social and regulatory legislation called the Progressive movement.

In reality this was a series of initially unrelated movements aimed at controlling evils created by advancing industrialism and its corollary, urbanism. On the one hand big business was steadily attacked by reformers as the symbol of ruthless competition and too great concentration of private power; on the other, small business was even more harassed by social legislation and the increasing power of organized labor.

Just as the reformers lacked unity of aim, business lacked uniform reactions. Big business had relatively few contacts with small and medium-sized enterprise. The really big companies had head offices in the major metropolitan areas, and in the decade 1900–1910 only a few branch plants. In most cities medium-sized local enterprises dominated the business scene. Trade associations and organizations like the National Association of Manufacturers were supported by small business and neglected by the "trusts." As a result small business was at least complacent about attacks on the trusts and railroad regulation, while big business appears to have done little to help small business fight social legislation in the states.[9]

The battle against, and the minor effects of social legislation on small business were hard to estimate. As the advanced industrial states led in compelling workmen's compensation insurance, limiting hours, or forbidding child labor, this legislation became one of the forces driving business to the South where such laws scarcely existed before 1914. Against this trend were higher freight rates in the southern area and loss of close contact with customers and suppliers. A satisfactory analysis would require research so far unattempted.

The Progressive attack upon the trusts revived and continued the pressures of earlier decades. The period 1897–1903 was the most important for industrial mergers and consolidations in United States history, and many people became fearful as to where the trend was leading. Professor C. J. Bullock of Harvard wrote in 1901: "If experience ever demonstrates that the arguments of many economists are correct then we shall be confronted with the grim fact that competition is dead and that monopoly is inevitable in most important branches of manufacturing industry." [10] Desiring to prove the government's power to deal with the situation, President Theodore Roosevelt ordered his Attorney General to start prosecutions against some of the larger monopolies. The resulting Supreme Court decisions in the Northern Securities and Standard Oil cases led to further exposition of the meaning of the Sherman Act of 1890.

In the first of these cases (1904), the Court ruled that the intent and result of the formation of the New Jersey holding company for Great Northern and Northern Pacific Railroads were an illegal combination in restraint of interstate commerce, and that no state, simply by creating a corporation, could prevent Congress from exercising its power to regulate commerce. "The power to deal with industrial monopoly and suppress it," exulted President Roosevelt, "was thus restored . . . " [11]

But what were the meanings of "restrain" and "monopolize" in the law? In the Standard Oil case of 1911, the Court abandoned the doctrine that a monopoly of manufacture was not directly a monopoly of commerce, as had been set forth in 1895 in the American Sugar Refining case, and held that it must use its own judgment in deciding whether monopolies were in harmful restraint of trade. Applying this "rule of reason," the Court ordered Standard Oil to be broken up into certain constituent companies. Justice John Marshall Harlan dissented from the assumption of discretionary power by the Court. "This statement," he wrote, "surprises me quite as much as would a statement that black was white or white was black . . . One thing is certain, the 'rule of reason,' to which the Court refers, does not justify the perversion of the plain words of an act in order to defeat the will of Congress." [12]

Equally incensed by the decision, Progressives and Democrats demanded a stronger law. As a result the Clayton Act was passed in 1914. Whereas the Sherman Act had used general and sweeping language, the framers of the Clayton Act sought specifically to prohibit the practices that led to the control of markets. The law condemned price discriminations, exclusive selling or leasing contracts, the acquisition of stock in one corporation by another or the combination of two corporations through stock ownership, or interlocking directorships in two or more corporations any one of which had over a million dollars in capital. But each prohibition was limited to cases where the result would be substantially to lessen competition or tend to create a monopoly. While the bill was denounced in the Senate as "the greatest victory of a legislative nature that has been won by the trusts and combinations within the life-time of any man," [13] it added somewhat to the restraints on corporate activity. Furthermore, another act of the same session created the Federal Trade Commission, charged with enforcing the Clayton Act and preventing unfair competition. This Commission was expected to enforce the antitrust laws in the same way that the Interstate Commerce Commission enforced laws relating to the railroads.

The Clayton Act specifically exempted trade unions and farmer coöperatives, in the proper pursuance of their functions, from its provisions. Later laws such as the Capper-Volstead Act of 1922 and the Cooperative Marketing Act of 1926 strengthened the immunities of agricultural organizations. Meanwhile, the Webb-Pomerene Act of 1918 placed combinations for foreign trade beyond the reach of antitrust laws.

The federal court decisions from 1914 to 1930 continued to emphasize the fact that the antitrust laws were to be seen as barriers against the continuation of overly oppressive forms of monopoly rather than criminal legislation for the effective punishment of all those who conspired to restrain trade. In 1912 a district court handed down prison sentences for flagrant violations of the Sherman Act by officers of the National Cash Register Company, but higher courts set the judgment aside, and the company settled by paying some insignificant costs and promising to be good in the future. In the United States Steel case, which dragged on for a decade and finally brought about a Supreme Court decision in 1920, it was ruled that size did not in itself violate the law if the big company appeared to act in the public interest. Opponents of the decision held that this substituted the "rule of business expediency" for the "rule of reason" announced in the Standard Oil case of 1911. In a series of trade association cases in the early twenties, the Supreme Court ended up by ruling that exchange of prices and other information among competitors was legal if not carried on for the explicit purpose of raising prices. During the twenties, Republican attorneys general instituted relatively few antitrust actions, and, as Professor William Z. Ripley put it, the Federal Trade Commission tried to commit hara-kiri.

Forty years of antitrust laws had failed to restore anything approaching "pure" competition. But except in some agricultural markets, pure competition had probably never existed save in the theories of economists. The federal laws had served to define certain rules for "monopolistic" competition. A few companies could share a market and fix prices so long as they did not do this by written agreements, or take overt action to prevent new competitors from entering the field. The laws dictated a live-and-let-live policy among the largest firms, since attempts by them to devour each other might lead to prosecution. Although such arrangements lacked the efficiency of monopoly, where advertising and duplicated services could be reduced, and probably produced prices higher than under more effective competition, the situation seemed, on the whole, to satisfy the public. It was doubtful whether most Americans wanted to see General Motors or General Electric broken up into smaller units, and even more doubtful that they wanted a single automobile trust with the concommitant need for strict federal regulation.

### THE AREA OF BIG BUSINESS

The spectacular and portentous aspects of the activities of the corporate giants magnified their role in the American economy. To many Americans at the turn of the century, the Rockefellers, Goulds, Guggenheims, and a score of others, appeared to run the economy and to be gaining rapidly in power. W. J. Ghent, a socialist, predicted that the United States would succumb to a benevolent feudalism run by big business.

For some years the growth of big companies was very rapid. In 1897 there were only eight industrial companies with over fifty million dollars in capital; by 1903 there were forty such giants. But, outside of small-scale household production, there were also over two hundred thousand manufacturing enterprises and a total of about one million two hundred thousand business concerns. Even if companies with five million dollars in capital, whether in transportation, finance, or manufacturing, were considered as "big," the total number of such companies in the first decade of the twentieth century was well under one thousand. Their policy-making executive employees probably numbered less than fifty thousand men, compared with perhaps two million proprietors and managers of small business.

In general the areas dominated by big businesses, such as railroad and traction companies, public utilities, iron and steel, smelting and refining, farm equipment, electrical equipment, and oil refining, were those in which small business had either never existed or had been superseded at an early stage. Many contemporary writers and later historians wrote of the loss of opportunity for the little man in business, but there is no such literature from businessmen themselves. Since the beginning of industrialism there had been a gradual growth in the size of the average firm. This meant that for manufacturing more capital was necessary for a successful start. But this difficulty seems to have been readily overcome by the increasing level of savings by those in upper-income groups, and greater familiarity with industrial risks by both bankers and private investors.

The area in which opportunity was declining was agriculture, not business. In each generation there were more businesses of all types, small, large, and medium, in relation to the population, and fewer people working on farms. Boys interested in business, therefore, had not only an opportunity to go into an increasing number of different enterprises for themselves, but had in addition the choice of a career in a big corporation.

Furthermore, the rapid growth in bigness that had caused alarm in the late nineties and early years of the new century slacked off. According to Berle and Means' calculations, the gross assets of the two hundred largest nonfinancial corporations increased in dollar value only 68 per cent between 1909 and 1919, whereas the general price level advanced over 80 per cent.[14] In the twenties the two hundred largest nonfinancial corporations grew more rapidly in assets and income than the smaller companies but still fell far short of being the norm of economic activity in the United States. Even if the next 800 nonfinancial corporations were included, which in 1929 covered companies with gross assets over twenty million, the group did a relatively small part of the nation's total business in dollars, and employed perhaps one man in six. In point of numbers of enterprises small and medium-sized businesses more than held their own. The number of firms listed by Dun and Bradstreet increased from about one million two hundred thousand in 1900 to over two million by 1930, a rate of growth faster than that of the nation's population. Monopoly capitalism or "benevolent feudalism" was developing, if at all, at a gradual pace.

Yet able scholars like A. A. Berle, Jr. held and continued to hold that the two hundred nonfinancial corporations which in 1929 did only about 40 per cent of the corporate business dominated the economy.[15] The basis for this apparent paradox is the importance given to manufacturing, railroad transportation, and public utilities. From 1900 on these areas had been the realm of big business. But they did not represent a majority of the opportunities for employment, and the areas open to new enterprise continued to increase. The crucial point in the argument was thus the control exercised by big business over the rest of the economy.

On this question opinions differed widely throughout the first part of the century, and the real situation was difficult to assess. Were wholesalers dominated by the producers? Were mass-produced manufactured goods more important to the economy than food and a hundred kinds of service? Were the few big concerns that did about half the manufacturing a dominant influence on the thousands that did the other half? Discussion based on present information cannot answer these questions, but it may prevent stereotyped answers.

The movement to restrict competition in price was not confined to big business. All highly capitalized concerns wanted price stability and the growing interest of professional management in long-run security produced wide support for the medieval or mercantilist idea of "just price." This implied the end of secret price cutting and the adoption of uniform trade practices. As A. J. Eddy, a Chicago lawyer, wrote in 1912 in a book called *The New Competition:*

> The basis of the old competition is secrecy, the strength of the new is knowledge: the essence of the old is deceit, the spirit of the new is truth. Concealment characterizes all the dealings of the old; frankness is vital to the new.
>
> The old looks with suspicious eye on all associations and combinations; without cooperation the new is impossible.[16]

In industries dominated by a few large companies informal understandings usually led to satisfactory coöperation in pricing. Steel prices were set for a numer of years at annual dinners held by Judge Gary of United States Steel. When rival firms started cutting prices in 1908, they were warned that if they resorted to "unreasonable and destructive competition" they would compel the "application of the law of the survival of the fittest."[17] Licensing of patents between competing companies was another means of controlling prices and conditions of sale. But in the group of industries in which competition was not restrained by either large firms or patents, uniformity required some type of formal action.

The trade association was the obvious agency for putting Eddy's principles into practice. By 1912 there were both regional and national trade associations for most industries, but some of them were not very active. A number of them now started to exchange information about costs, prices, orders, and inventories. The purported aim was to "coordinate competitive forces without relinquishing the fruits that spring from individual initiative."[18] During World War I the government's use of the associations as agencies to estimate, apportion, and stimulate production strengthened the existing groups and aided the formation of new ones. By the end of the war there were perhaps one thousand trade associations operating on a nation-wide basis, and 10 or 15 per cent of these were experimenting with open-price policy. Under this system each member posted its prices with the association, which in turn circulated them, along with pertinent information, in letters or periodicals.

Insofar as the new competition was effective it had unforeseen results on other aspects of economic life. Previously, swings of the business cycle had been accompanied by wide fluctuations in prices; now these shifts from buyers' to sellers' markets, or the reverse, caused less change in prices and more in the volume of production. With better control of the market producers could reduce the supply to what could be sold at about the existing prices. This situation in turn meant more unemployment in depressions but better maintenance of wages for those still employed, and less total income for the firm but better assurance of profits and dividends. Economists began to talk of "sticky" prices and wages as "rigidities" in the business structure. And as business lost elasticity, depressions appeared to be losing some of their former tendency toward self-correction.

Prices that could be controlled were said to be "administered" by management. This in turn changed the character of the activities of top executives. Survival in price warfare had emphasized striving for efficiency and economy in production. Frugality and careful figuring were the watch-words. But success under a system of comfortably high, stable prices depended on gaining more of the market through ingenious advertising and selling. Cutting costs through attention to detail was less vital to the chief executive than ability for choosing the right product and understanding the market.

The new competition and its consequences were integral parts of the evolving pattern of large-scale industrialism. The very basis of mass production was the commitment of vast amounts of time and money to a particular way of doing a job. Blueprinting and manufacturing the machinery needed to fashion a new product could take two to four years. The need for careful advance planning, because of inability to change once the process was in motion, applied not only to machines and buildings, but to office work as well. A filing system might become obsolete, but to refile fifteen or twenty million letters, in, say, an insurance office, was as staggering a task as to retool completely an assembly line. Communication also had to be planned and routinized. The smooth functioning of a vast organization required established channels of information and control. But such elements introduced a time lag and a chance that an idea for improvement might get lost on the way. Even a well-received suggestion entering at the bottom of the managerial hierarchy might take two years to work its way to the top and then back to the point where it could be translated into action.

The old-time owner-manager's goal of gaining an advantage over competitors by innovating and secretly developing new ways of doing things became largely meaningless in the big company. There could be few important "trade secrets" where hundreds of men had to be informed and where new methods could only be introduced after long testing and preparation. One company might be more progressive than another in putting the new into practice, but rarely were its ideas unknown to competitors.

### THE NEW-STYLE HOLDING COMPANY

In spite of the important changes in technology, size, and methods of operation, no basically new development in the legal structure of firms took place in the first half of the twentieth century. Proprietorships, partnerships, simple corporations, and holding companies continued to be the forms for carrying on the nation's business activities. But the holding company was used in new ways that promised for a time to be of great significance. The early holding companies, mostly chartered under the New Jersey general act of 1889, were usually of the single-stage variety. The parent company owned stock in a number of operating subsidiaries. In the twenties, however, circumstances led to the piling of one holding company on top of another to form a multistage or pyramided structure.

The pyramid allowed the directors of the top company to control more real assets with the same amount of venture capital, or to attract more capital from the investing public without endangering the directors' complete control of the system. The mechanics of the structure depended upon the fact that a bare majority, or even less, of the voting stock of a corporation carried control of all of its operations and assets. In Samuel Insull's utility pyramid, for example, each of his dollars invested in Corporation Securities Company of Chicago ("Corps" for short), might control over two thousand dollars' worth of assets in an operating company at the base, such as Georgia Power and Light. This so-called "leverage" depended, of course, on the fact that the public was willing to buy the securities of all the intermediate, nonoperating companies. During the 1920's, investors were not only willing but eager to "get in" on this fast-growing industry without questioning the soundness or practicality of the corporate set-up.

In practice most of these structures soon ceased to be orderly pyramids proceeding from many operating companies at the base through intermediate holding companies to one parent corporation at the top. The companies borrowed from each other, bought each other's securities as well as those of outside corporations, issued bonds, and often produced a tangle of intercompany ownership that defied comprehension. Owen D. Young, lawyer and Chairman of the Board of General Electric, said of the Insull public-utility pyramid: "It is impossible for any man to grasp the situation of that vast structure . . . it was so set up that you could not possibly get an accounting system that would not mislead even the officers themselves." [19]

The depression of the thirties discredited pyramided holding companies. When falling revenues forced reorganizations, they were shown to be overcapitalized and financially mismanaged. As a result, they became anathema to investors, and the federal government in the Public Utility Holding Act of 1935 placed so many restrictions on such companies that most of them were forced to release their subsidiaries. In the sad and realistic thirties new pyramids appeared unprofitable. After the spectacular collapse of the Van Sweringen pyramid of trunk-line railroads, the Interstate Commerce Commission also came to frown on control acquired through complex financial structures.

The abuses of the holding company by empire-building financiers should not obscure its great value to big business as a legitimate means of organization. By this means companies could order their inner relations in several different ways. They might choose a unified form of organization, such as that of Du Pont or Ford, where subsidiaries, aside from those in foreign countries, exist to perform specific functions. Or they could design a federal type like General Motors, where considerable autonomy is allowed to the presidents of the producing units, but major policies are coördinated by staff committees of the parent company. A federated type allowing still more local autonomy is the Weyerhaeuser Timber Company, in which the top unit represents ownership but takes little direct part in the management of subsidiaries.

Whatever their type of organization, almost all large companies owned the stock of operating subsidiaries, just as American Telephone & Telegraph, for example, held that of the various state telephone companies. The top subsidiary companies might in turn own the stock of smaller firms set up for special purposes, but such stages were incidental to the effective control of operations and were not a financial device for increasing the leverage of some group of insiders in the topmost holding company.

### THE CONTROL OF BIG BUSINESS

It seemed inevitable that as corporations grew larger, there must be an increasing separation of ownership from active contol. The good securities market of the twenties encouraged families or small owning groups that controlled companies to sell stock to the public. Such sales paid for new additions, expanded working capital without borrowing from the banks,

permitted the old owners to diversify their holdings by buying into other companies, and increased the public interest
in the welfare of the company. By 1930 the management group
had come to be much less associated with ownership than in
the previous generation.

Increasing the numbers of stockholders diminished the possibility of any group of small stockholders overthrowing management. But also to gain security from raids by big market
operators some companies issued only nonvoting stock to the
public. This practice brought down the wrath of reformers
such as Professor William Z. Ripley, and numerous journalists. F.P.A. in his "Conning Tower" in the New York *World*
published "On Waiting for the *New Masses* to Denounce Nonvoting Stocks,"

> Then you who drive the fractious nail,
> And you who lay the heavy rail,
> And all who bear the dinner pail
>   And daily punch the clock —
> Shall it be said your hearts are stone?
> They are your brethren and they groan!
>   Oh, drop a tear for those who own
> Non-voting corporate stock.[20]

Even the Investment Banker's Association denounced the practice, and it was gradually abandoned. The great majority of
stockholders, however, had long since ceased to view their
companies as property they could administer, or their votes
as instruments of power.

The board of directors also ceased to be an effective representation of ownership. Only a few members of large company
boards kept well enough informed to take a hand in guiding
the organization, and these members were usually salaried
officers of the company. At the end of the nineteenth century,
salaried officers had feared the penetrating eye of a Rockefeller, Harriman, or Morgan on the board. Now, in the lush
twenties, with corporate savings adequate for company needs
and new capital easy to acquire, the salaried executives boldly

questioned the prerogatives of the directors. Management developed the theory that the director's function was merely advisory, that he should not try to form or veto policy or to interfere in the operation of the concern. This de-emphasis of the board as the elected representatives of the owners, as the supreme authority for which management worked as hired hands, reached its extreme in such boards as those of American Tobacco or Standard Oil of New Jersey, composed entirely of salaried officers. But on all large company boards, officers came to play the leading role.

Was this new assumption of authority a "managerial revolution" and was the new system of big business "managerial enterprise?" [21] By 1930 the answer to such questions was by no means clear. In routine matters the administrators certainly wielded the power, but in questions of financial policy board members representing banks or insurance companies might overrule management. While small stockholders could not, by themselves, organize to overturn the administration, big financiers who had acquired a large amount of stock might succeed in an appeal to the small stockholders to support their slate of directors.

Control, therefore, was generally shared by several of the directors and managers, the locus of authority depending upon the point at issue. The professional manager who, without investing any capital, had made his way up through the organization, and the board members who represented financial houses or family trusts were all presumably more interested in a strong, progressive, going concern than in paying unusually large dividends to stockholders. The president of the company, in theory its most important entrepreneur, was apt to be primarily interested in keeping a satisfactory balance among the various claimants to the company income. Those speaking for more wages for labor, higher salaries for management, better service for customers, adding to the company's cash reserves, improvement of the physical plant, or dividends for the stock holders represented superficially contending interests in that if one got more in any given division, the others received less. In this situation it was not astonishing that the modern professional manager tended, perhaps unconsciously, to favor the financial claims of those who could bring more constant pressure than could the mass of stockholders. Such a situation meant, among other things, that successful large companies paid high wages and salaries, accumulated substantial reserves against depreciation or depression, invested sizable sums in research, and paid relatively low dividends.

### THE SCIENCE OF BUSINESS ADMINISTRATION

The growing size of companies created new problems from bottom to top. At the bottom, the old contact between owner-manager and skilled craftsmen was lost. Large plants were run by professional managers who were below the top policy-making level of the company. Mass-production shops presented new problems in handling men and materials.

When Frederic W. Taylor set himself up as a professional management consultant in 1894, his business card read: "Systematizing Shop and Manufacturing Costs a Specialty." His program soon came to be known, both at home and abroad, as "scientific management." His general principle was "that in almost all of the mechanic arts the science which underlies each act of each workman is so great and amounts to so much that the workman who is best suited to actually doing the work is incapable of fully understanding this science, without the guidance and help of those who are working with him or over him." [22]

In Taylor's system foremen had to study the essential motions and the minimum time for each job and then instruct the worker. The faster rate that resulted would be maintained by pay increases for productivity. To gain deeper insight some foremen should specialize in supervision of certain functions rather than in complete management of a small number of men. More supervisors might be required, but they would be paid for by greatly increased output.

Although no company adopted all of Taylor's ideas at once, many started experimenting with them, and still others paid increasing attention to shop management. When Louis D. Brandeis, later a Justice of the Supreme Court, told the Interstate Commerce Commission that the railroads could save one million dollars by scientific management, "it was like a shot heard around America." [23] In the years before World War I, Taylorism was discussed by all types of industrialists, and Taylor had many imitators, each with his own system. A major deterrent to the adoption of such schemes was the opposition of workers. The fear, often realized, that piece rates or other incentives would not be maintained once production speeded up, led labor to disregard the instructions of "efficiency experts."

The shortage of labor during and immediately after World War I produced the new "science" of personnel management, designed to find the right man for the job and to keep him working at it. A flood of seemingly learned books appeared, and "experts" were hired at good salaries, but with the depression of the early twenties and a surplus of workers, this early enthusiasm for scientific personnel work subsided.

As some companies came to have thousands of administrators, it became clear that business was encountering the same types of problems that had existed for centuries in public administration. As one well-qualified critic saw it, business growth had "resulted in concentrating in relatively few hands a degree and scope of economic power which transcends the limits of effective administration." [24] Whether or not this was true, business needed its own political science.

Pursuit of a science of administration led to better cost-accounting techniques, an increase of middle management and an increased use of staff consultants. After World War I, alert companies hired industrial engineers, theoretical economists, and other specialists who might provide new knowledge of or perspective on business problems. In order to guard against or prepare for disruptive changes in technology, big companies established research laboratories employing scores of scientists. Increasingly complex relations with both government and organized labor necessitated more legal experts to analyze proposed legislation, more trained lobbyists or public-relations men to forestall harmful bills, and more reliable analysts to learn or forecast government policy.

At the top level, that of chairmen, presidents, and major vice-presidents, the problems of business administration seemed most difficult of all. The inefficiencies of single departments or weak administrators might be detected and eliminated by careful accounting or staff reports, but how were men to be trained, selected, and inspired to undertake the task of coördinating and directing the enterprise as a whole? How were men to translate power into effective administration?

The rise of the university business school was one effort to provide the proper training. The first of these, the Wharton School at the University of Pennsylvania, was founded in 1884; a few others, such as the Graduate School of Business Administration at Harvard, preceded World War I; but the great increase came in the twenties. By the end of the decade most large universities were offering undergraduate or graduate courses both in the essential techniques of business and in academic subjects that might contribute to sounder and broader executive viewpoints.

No scholar, however, found an acceptable system for choosing executives. Methods of selection remained largely rule of thumb, and as organizations grew bigger, success for the man without influential connections depended on recognition of his abilities by someone in top management, usually through a fortunate conjunction of circumstances. The individual competitive struggle for success in such companies, therefore, took the form of means for attracting attention to one's desirable qualities of loyalty, coöperation, intelligence, and leadership rather than the quest for wealth or market advantages.

The change that had taken place in the road to success can be illustrated by comparing Andrew Carnegie's instructions to young men of the late nineteenth century with those of a twentieth-century railroad president. "Is there any would-be businessman before me," Carnegie asked a group of Cornell students, "content in forecasting his future, to figure himself as labouring all his life for a fixed salary? Not one, I am sure.

In this you have the dividing line between business and non-businesss; the one is a master, and depends on profits, the other a servant and depends upon salary . . . I do not believe that even the presidents of these corporations, being only salaried men, are to be . . . classed as strictly businessmen at all." When a man is to be made a partner, "then comes the question of questions, *is he honest and true?*" Among rules for getting ahead Carnegie advised: "Boss your boss just as soon as you can; try it on early. There is nothing he will like so well if he is the right kind of boss; if he is not, he is not the man for you to remain with — leave him whenever you can, even at a present sacrifice, and find one capable of discerning genius." [25]

In the 1940's a young boy wrote to a railroad president who was approaching retirement age, asking how to get a job like his. The president replied, "Industry and cooperation are very important . . . Teamwork is as essential on a railroad as it is on a football field . . . Cultivate and develop a pleasing and friendly personality . . . Show an interest in other people and what they have to say . . . finish college . . . " The president concluded: "Of course, opportunity and good fortune also play a part." [26]

Actually, there was nothing new in the evolving big-business situation. Men in the bureaucracies of Egypt, Greece, and Rome had striven for success under somewhat similar conditions, but the turn toward an organizational career for the country's most ambitious citizens was a notable departure from historic American conditions and conflicted with a good deal of the nation's cultural heritage. Americans had tended to see themselves as self-reliant, aggressive enterprisers rather than smoothly polished negotiators. The subtleties of approach and fine manners of Europeans had been sources of ridicule; now they seemed to pave the road to success.

While the top executives of the large companies continued to talk the language of earnings for the stockholders and to keep their formal behavior oriented toward profits, most of them had relatively little direct stake in the size of the dividends paid by their companies. Maximization of profits was the orthodox slogan, but one that for management probably lacked much emotional force. From the earliest days executives of large corporations affected with a public interest, such as railroads, had been in favor of steady but moderate profits rather than sheer maximization.[27] The attitude that secure profits over a long period were more desirable than large and risky returns came to be generally held by twentieth-century management.[28]

What then were the personal incentives of executives once they had reached the probable top of the promotional ladder? A general answer appeared to be "the continual stimulation that derives from the pleasure of immediate accomplishment." [29] The president of a big company, asked why he didn't stop work on a holiday, replied: "I'm not working, I'm having fun." [30] The achievements from executive effort were made more satisfactory by the admiration of one's peers in business or by significant groups of the outside public. Thus achievement for its own sake, the wielding of socially accepted power, and personal prestige were generally more important incentives than either increases in salary or company profits, as such.[31]

Many companies, however, sought to substitute for personal profit financial incentives such as bonus plans and management funds. As did most other developments of the managerial system, the earliest of these plans antedated World War I, but they were particularly characteristic of the prosperous twenties. Part of the year's earnings would be divided among the administrators on either a fixed percentage, or by vote of the board of directors or the chief officers. In good years, like 1928 and 1929, these payments might greatly exceed the regular salary of the executive, and a few companies paid bonuses even in 1932. Plans for buying of stock by management ran counter to a desire for wise diversification of personal investment in order to achieve added individual security which was likely to impel officers to hold only a reasonable amount of stock in the companies for which they worked. The fact that some companies adopted bonus and stock purchase plans and other equally progressive schemes, did not indicate that such developments were solutions to the problem of stimulating energy and devotion to the company.

Intracompany competition and ratings by accounting controls were more positive ways of insuring efficiency. General Motors cars, for example, were in competition with each other, and their factory and marketing costs could be compared. Success on such a basis could accrue without large profits. During the depression of the thirties the officers of Cadillac won high prestige for not losing money when other cars of the same price range were all showing large losses. "Book" competition could be rigorous in companies like American Telephone & Telegraph, which had similar operations all over the nation. Accountants could readily check with great precision the efficiency of a local management group, but it was hard to measure the ability of any single individual.

In order to counteract the centrifugal forces of internecine warfare between the companies of General Motors, President Alfred P. Sloan in the 1920's developed a system of coördination through committees made up of board members and officers of the various constituent companies.[32] Thus the company appeared to have the best of two worlds, the incentives of competition and the efficiencies of semimonopoly.

Increasing levels of security and prestige were also incentives for the executive of the big company. Personal recognition could be given through larger offices, more prerogatives, and higher titles that carried prestige in the community as well as in the company. In this way the need for labeling officials in a large formal organization could also be used to improve morale.

Railroads started conferring the title of vice-president on the man in charge of each part of the business, such as traffic, operation, maintenance, or finance, in the mid-nineteenth century, but other large companies were slow to follow this practice until after 1900. Then spurred somewhat by ideas of scientific management, and still more by the demands of increasing size, companies added numerous specialized officials with titles ranging from assistant superintendent to senior vice-president. As holding companies spread there also came to be scores of officerships in subsidiaries. "In the last forty years or so," said the President of International Harvester in 1953, "this system has developed from what football coaches would call a one platoon system to something that approximates a thirty or forty platoon system in industry." [33]

By 1930 a big company might have from five to fifty vice-presidents of the parent organization and an equally large number of assistant vice-presidents as well as assistant secretaries and assistant treasurers. There might also be assistants to the chairman of the board, the president, and vice-presidents. Usually these assistants were staff officers, that is, specialists or roving executives who handled particular types of problems or else improved communication and knit the organization together. The subsidiaries would have their presidents, vice-presidents, and other officers. Often the chief officers of the parent company divided among themselves the topmost posts in the subsidiaries, but the lesser positions were filled by additional officer personnel.

Under the officers in rank, but not always in salary, were managers, superintendents, department heads, agents, supervisors, and their various assistants. Although no exact research has been done on the question, it seems probable that the increase in administrators kept up with the growing quantity of business, or in other words, that there was not much saving in cost per unit of product in administrative salaries and expense accounts as volume increased.

As in the granting of titles, business needs could be combined with better morale through officers' clubs. The club was generally built around a comfortable restaurant where the staff could assemble for lunch and use their leisure time for informal discussion of company problems. In many companies officers also spent much of their social life entertaining each other, and talking shop over highballs. By such means the company might become an engrossing interest in both work and recreation. A later report on the habits of big company officials noted that, "In many instances . . . executives look upon the office day as something of an interruption in their actual work." [34] So far did this tendency go in some companies that an opposite danger began to develop, that of losing the perspective of the outsider and viewing problems only in terms of group clichés. The dilemma is inherent in group activity. The somewhat introverted individualist fertile in new ideas tends to coöperate poorly and to disrupt the smooth functioning of the organization, while the outgoing type, hungry for the friendship and support of his fellows, may coöperate excellently but lack the ability to innovate. Many critics inside the ranks of business thought that the big company tended to advance too many men of this latter type.

The problems of prestige, security, and morale ran from top to bottom of the large company. "You will learn to your sorrow," wrote John L. McCaffrey, "that, while a drill press never sulks and a drop hammer never gets jealous of other drop hammers, the same cannot be said for people . . . The man in the middle of the management pyramid, however, neither makes the decisions nor carries them out. He finds it easy to feel that his judgment was neither sought nor honored . . . He often feels, and frequently says, that he is just a high-priced office boy." [35]

The routine administrator was given a feeling of added importance in several ways. For workers and lower management the company magazine and company club were means to both individual distinction and closer group coöperation. Company magazines devoted to internal news began as early as the 1870's, but there were only about thirty-five in 1916. Between that date and 1921 the number increased tenfold and grew steadily thereafter. By 1925 practically all of the three or four hundred biggest corporations had some type of house organ.[36]

These magazines reported promotions, social events, athletic contests, marriages, and other family news. They published fiction and poetry by company employees. Editorially they served as media for indoctrination in company policy and ideals. The fact that there was a company reading public or community also gave a feeling of added importance and responsibility to the chief executive officers.

Company clubs achieved some of these same purposes. Salaried employees were given a chance to build friendships and become recognized personalities within the company atmosphere. In some companies workers and managers mingled at the golf course or bowling alleys, although upper management was inclined to avoid these contacts.

### THE LARGE COMPANY IN SOCIETY

While some of the internal problems of bigness were being met by new devices, external relations became more complex than ever before. From 1910 on, state regulatory laws affecting labor and factory conditions in various industries multiplied, and commissions were established to set rates for public utilities. For many businesses World War I produced complex relations with the federal government that were not always happily resolved. And events in Europe gave a portent of more government regulation to come.

Legitimizing or justifying to the public the great power exercised by the managers of big business offered theoretical as well as practical difficulties. The values of managerial trusteeship and social responsibility were common justifications, but carried too far they could be a rationale for socialization.[37] Service to the consumer, based on the theory that consumers exercised ultimate sovereignty and would punish weak managements by loss of patronage, was another justification for the existence of successful ones. But no over-all principle, as basic and satisfactory as direct competition had been in classic business doctrine, was developed by the new controllers of big companies.

Even if the basic creed of management still lacked clarity, knowledge of ways to create public opinion favorable to business enterprise had grown greatly. Looking back over the period from the vantage point of 1929, Ernest Elmo Calkins, an advertising man, wrote: "The war taught us the new possibilities of molding public opinion, improved the machinery and transformed the old-time press agent into the modern public relations counsel, whose clients are colleges, cathedrals, corporations, societies, and even nations." [38]

Before World War I, Ivy Lee had acted in the role of a public-relations counselor, most notably in building a more favorable picture of the Rockefeller family after the Colorado Fuel and Iron Company strike in 1914; but President Wilson's Committee on Public Information became the great training school. John Price Jones, later famous as a fund raiser, and Edward L. Bernays, the most important innovator of the 1920's, both served on this committee under the chairmanship of ex-newspaper man George Creel. Here the most modern psychological ideas (Bernays was Sigmund Freud's nephew) were combined with activities on a scale never dreamed of by earlier publicity men. Two years after the war Creel wrote of the operation as *How We Advertised America.*[39]

By 1921 both Lee and Bernays were using the phrase "public relations," and big companies were setting up publicity or public-relations departments, in some cases headed by what were derisively called "good-will" or "luncheon" vice-presidents.[40] As Colonel Stewart of Standard Oil saw it: "If you don't have the public for you, a seriously large part of it is likely to be against you, and no business can continue to exist successfully unless a large part of the public is for it." [41]

These public-relations efforts of the twenties were still on what would later be regarded as an elementary level. They depended to a large extent on "puff" news items sent to editors, articles signed by important businessmen and planted in mass-circulation periodicals, and advertising designed to create good will. Public lectures, popular company or industry histories, and moving pictures also came into use. The telephone company was a leader in the use of moving pictures. Between 1926 and 1935, the company produced fifty-six public-information films. The director of the bureau at American Telephone & Telegraph said that theater managers were willing to show these films, because the manager could "see for himself that they are purely informative and educational and will not detract from his program of entertainment." [42] By 1929 the Bell System estimated that during the year 52,932,796 people had attended 131,696 showings of the company films.[43]

In spite of the apparently advanced methods of such companies, the general philosophy of public relations was that of seizing upon some overt act that would reveal the company in a favorable light rather than reforming the basic policies of the company in such a way as gradually to win public favor. The "two-way street" aspect of public relations had not as yet been accepted.[44]

In the postwar decade the stockholders were recognized as an important group for improving public relations. A few shares might make their holder a loyal supporter against public criticism or government encroachments. As a result, a number of large companies, particularly the public utilities, carried on campaigns to increase both the number and geographical spread of small stockholders. American Telephone & Telegraph, for example, by selling stock to both the public and its own employees through its local offices, increased the number of stockholders owning five shares or less from some 50,000 in 1920 to 210,000 in 1930.[45]

Now the stockholder came to be seen as a friend to be cultivated rather than a troublesome critic to be avoided. Public-relations men turned their attention to giving the stockholder a better impression of the company. Presidents were persuaded to sign letters welcoming new members to the stockholder family; other letters conveyed special news; magazines, previously used for internal morale building, were made more attractive and sent to the stockholders; and annual reports became more detailed and persuasive. The intelligent stockholder might recognize that none of these devices could tell him much about the prospects of his investment in a big organization, but they undoubtedly aroused stockholder interest in the company which in turn produced some degree of identification with company problems. The new public relations demonstrated that more big companies were coming to see themselves as organizations that could not avoid social and political issues.

# 5

# The Era of the Bankers

By the early twentieth century many scholars and journalists believed that during their lifetime capitalism in the Western world had fallen under the control of bankers and financiers. Following a line of reasoning expressed particularly by German economic historians, these analysts saw capitalism as going through a series of stages. The mercantile stage, in which America had grown up, was characterized by the importing and exporting merchant as the most important type of entrepreneur. This stage was superseded in the early nineteenth century by industrial capitalism, with independent small-scale factory proprietors as the dynamic or formative influence. As business grew larger and more corporate, the need for raising capital from the investing public brought the investment banker into prominence until by 1900 he was conceived to be the most important figure in a stage called finance capitalism.

### THE RISE OF INVESTMENT BANKERS

The last stage in this theory appeared to be well exemplified in the United States. The rapid growth of big business after the Civil War brought an increasing volume of large-scale security offerings in a market where capital for investment was relatively scarce. Competing with many attractive forms of local investment that could be supervised personally by the investor, shares or bonds in remote enterprises were difficult

79

to sell. Only the large investment firm with many contacts at home and abroad could readily dispose of a five- or ten-million-dollar issue.

Consequently, about a dozen large investment banking houses took over the initial underwriting of the financial needs of American big business. As might be expected in a situation where there were many companies seeking money and only a few powerful wholesalers of securities, the investment houses set the rules of the trade. By the nineties it was generally understood that there should be no shopping around or bargaining from one banker to the next.

The bankers regarded their relation to the enterprises that contracted for their aid in much the same light as the family doctor regarded his patients. The investment banker floated the original securities that brought the corporation, conceived in a charter, into actual life. When more money was needed for the growth of the young company, the same banker expected to be consulted about securing the sustenance. He prescribed the arrangements for corporate marriages and the creation of subsidiaries, and when, usually during depressions, the company became financially ill and could not meet its obligations, the banker recommended a plan for reorganization that would restore the patient to health. If corporate death occurred, through liquidation and the sale of assets at auction, the banker attended each phase of the proceedings, usually arranging for purchase of the remains by a group of bondholders.

For the marketing of sizable security issues the underwriting house would associate other large financial firms with itself in a syndicate. Each of the leading investment banks, such as J. P. Morgan; Kuhn, Loeb; Lee, Higginson; or Kidder, Peabody, had a group of "retail" outlets through which most of the securities reached the public. Banks, trust companies, and brokerage houses did the retail selling, but banks and trust and insurance companies also bought for their own investment portfolios. Consequently, it was important for the investment bankers to exercise influence in the affairs of these other financial institutions. In addition, considerable parts of the issue might be sold through coöperating investment houses, "correspondents" in London, Paris, Amsterdam, Berlin or other foreign money markets. Each of the big American firms, therefore, had to have important European correspondents or agencies. This somewhat informal world financial network led to the term, generally used invidiously, "international bankers."

### THE NEW YORK FINANCIAL COMMUNITY

At the same time that the public marketing of securities was increasing the business influence of the investment houses, the concentration of the head offices of large companies in New York City was adding greatly to the size and power of a few commercial banks. From the deposits of oil, meat, and metal producers, the National City Bank, which had always specialized in the financing of raw materials, rose to a leading position in city and nation. With resources of $200,000,000, a gold reserve second only to that of the United States Treasury, and deposits from some 200 inland banks, the influence of National City and of its president, James Stillman, approached that of a European central bank. Smaller in size, but almost equal in the financial importance of its chief depositors from the fields of railroads and industry, was the First National Bank of New York presided over by George F. Baker.

In addition to other metropolitan banks and trust companies, the four major life insurance companies were located in New York. Trust companies and life insurance companies were particularly good customers of investment bankers. Both could legally buy a considerable range of securities, and both were expanding their resources rapidly.

Inevitably the major sellers of securities, the great commercial bankers, and important depositors were drawn together, and the vigorous personality and sweeping financial ideas of J. Pierpont Morgan gave a structure and force to this community of interest that it might otherwise have lacked. As early as the late 1870's, he began to display his readiness to undertake big and difficult financial ventures. He had the ability to get rivals to coöperate, and when they would not he was prepared to act by himself. Having failed in the early nineties to get railroadmen to control competition by voluntary agreements, he seized the opportunity offered by the ensuing depression to reorganize several regional railroad networks, and place his representatives on their boards. Believing that coöperation was the life of sound finance, he brought about a number of mergers in the industrial field, creating such giants as General Electric, United States Steel, International Harvester, and International Mercantile Marine.

In some of these activities, other well-established houses, such as Kuhn, Loeb and Company, appeared as competitors, but Morgan succeeded in creating close relations with Stillman and Baker. He and his partners also controlled the Bankers and Guaranty Trust Companies and bought strategic shares of stock in the major life insurance companies. Access to these great "pooled savings" gave Morgan and other big investment bankers unprecedented ability to dispose of new securities; anyone denied such connections could scarcely find a sufficient buying public for large issues.

The Morgan–First National–National City financial group and the other old investment houses were not the only big interests in Wall Street. The same upsurge of inland production that had built up the great metropolitan banks had also produced many new general entrepreneurs — that is, men who controlled many companies, but whose occupation was buying, selling, and coördinating such ventures rather than taking an active part in routine management. Great mine owners like the Guggenheims or Thomas Fortune Ryan, and smaller and more speculative financiers like F. Augustus Heinze, Charles W. Morse, or Edward R. Thomas controlled banks and entered into large financial operations outside the more sedate and socially select sphere of the leading international bankers.

The panic of 1907 gave the Morgan interests a chance to strengthen their leadership and to weaken the influence of some of these financiers outside the fold. Following a stock-market panic on Wednesday, October 16, centering around the favorite stocks of Heinze, Morse, Thomas, and their allies, depositors started mass withdrawals from the banks of these speculators. Unable to meet these "runs" they appealed to the leaders of the banking community for aid. But the National City–First National–Morgan forces would not approve aid to these banks until their "objectionable" officers or directors were eliminated. As fear spread among all depositors, poorly managed trust companies were in difficulties. Morgan, returning from the annual conference of Episcopal bishops at Richmond, marshalled the resources of the financial group that he considered respectable. When a reliable examiner interrupted him in conference with Baker and Stillman to say that the Trust Company of America, then under heavy pressure from depositors, was solvent, Morgan said: "This, then, is the place to stop this trouble." [1] His word turned out to be the law. He dragooned unwilling bank presidents into subscribing funds for emergency loans, and also used millions lent by the Secretary of the Treasury to supply liquid funds for approved banks and trust companies.

By the end of the two weeks of crisis the elderly Morgan had demonstrated his leadership of American finance. Great individual financiers, such as the Rockefellers, E. H. Harriman, other big investment houses, and the presidents of the two leading commercial banks, had all accepted Morgan's leadership and supported his policies. Furthermore, the coöperative activities of the conservative leaders in the period of crisis appeared to have established a community of interest that continued in later years. In fact, to some outsiders it appeared to be a dangerous money trust.

### THE MONEY TRUST

Whether or not it could be called a trust, the picture of Wall Street financial arrangements disclosed by the Pujo Committee of the House of Representatives in 1913 showed concentrated financial controls in major areas of the American economy. Because of its apparent dominance of American big business and of the subtle character of financial influence, the Morgan–Baker–Stillman entente deserves careful analysis. To begin with, influence was exerted through representatives of the banking group on the boards of directors of various financial, utility, railroad and manufacturing concerns. Except where trustees held the stock, as for example in the Southern Railroad, the group representatives were not a majority of the board, and usually numbered only one or two members. Clearly such control as existed was a matter of influence, not absolute power.

The Pujo Committee decided that the House of Morgan, the First National Bank, the National City Bank, and the two Morgan-controlled trust companies, Bankers and Guaranty, constituted a distinct inner or policy-making group, apart from the broader sphere of financial coöperation which included other large investment banking houses such as August Belmont, Kidder, Peabody, and Lee, Higginson. The firm members or directors of the inner group held 118 directorships in thirty-four banks and trust companies, thirty-five directorships in ten insurance companies, and 193 directorships in sixty-eight non-financial corporations.[2] These 112 companies were among the largest in the nation.

But the members of these boards that belonged to the banking group made no systematic attempt to control or direct the big business activities of the nation. Even at the top the group operated with an informality unsuited to governing a business empire. Stillman often stopped in to see Baker and Morgan on the way to National City Bank. Occasionally they lunched together, but irregularly enough so that the meetings were arranged by an exchange of notes. By 1912 Stillman was spending most of his time in Europe. Aside from the chief officials of the separate institutions, each of whom had his regular duties to perform, there was no planning or fact-gathering group, and the lesser men were not called to meet as a joint board of strategy. Many of the 112 companies undoubtedly operated from 1900 to 1914 without any important guidance or restraint from those board members who, on the basis of the Pujo calculations, represented Morgan, Baker, and Stillman.

J. Pierpont Morgan, queried by Samuel Untermeyer for the

Pujo Committee late in 1912, denied that he exercised any great power or that such concentration of control existed. But George F. Baker talked more freely about the situation. Untermeyer said to him, "We are speaking of this concentration which has come about and the power it brings with it getting into the hands of very ambitious men, perhaps not overscrupulous. You see a peril in that, do you not?"

"Yes," replied Baker.

"So that safety," continued Untermeyer, "if you think there is safety in the situation, really lies in the personnel of the men."

"Very much."

"Do you think that is a comfortable situation for a great country to be in?"

"Not entirely."

Bankers outside the inner circle were more concerned. President Reynolds of the big Continental and Commercial Bank of Chicago testified: "I am inclined to think that the concentration having gone to the extent it has, does constitute a menace." [3] It seems likely that in most cases the pressure of the inner circle was exerted only in matters involving major financial commitments. The leading members of the group were burdened with too many directorships — partners of the House of Morgan alone held seventy-two — to take any account of the details of operation. But in financial matters the power of the banking representatives was far-reaching. As Charles Mellon, president of the New York, New Haven and Hartford Railroad said, where Mr. Morgan sat was the head of the board. [4] If the bankers of the country knew that Morgan, Baker, and Stillman were opposed to a certain policy, it might be virtually impossible for a company to finance it. Other bankers and financiers did not want to risk the long-run consequences of the antagonism of this powerful group.

In some instances the financial controls were operated forcefully. Morgan developed certain ideas which he wanted to see applied in important situations. He believed that stable corporate income could be secured by eliminating competition and securing a community of interest. Seeing company financial structure from the banker's standpoint, he was interested in protecting bondholders but relatively indifferent to the welfare of stockholders. In return for accepting lower interest rates, bondholders in reorganized companies were often given large blocks of common or preferred stock. Back of these policies, which increased total capitalization, seems to have been the belief that elimination of competition would allow adequate returns on the larger quantity of securities.

Sometimes these principles worked, especially during the prosperous years from 1897 to 1907, but when a region or an industry ceased growing and hard times came around, the Morgan capitalizations could cause new trouble. The New York, New Haven, and Hartford Railroad illustrated a major failure of the Morgan policies. J. Pierpont Morgan himself, as a member of the board, dictated a policy of buying competitors of all types, railroad, trolley, and boat, in order to secure a monopoly of through transportation in southern New England. Since Morgan's plans were soon well known, the prices were high. Had the region continued to grow rapidly, the New Haven might have been able to service the resulting additions to its bonded indebtedness. But after the panic of 1907 New England stagnated, and when a deep depression started early in 1913, the New Haven was unable to meet its fixed charges.

Other basic criticisms of the influence exercised by the Morgan–Baker–Stillman group are that it was unorganized, negative, and undemocratic. It did not lend itself to furthering higher productive efficiency or planning for risk-taking expansion. The views of the leaders were more inclined toward financial security than technological progress. Insofar as their influence was exerted in such matters it was likely to lead to the postponing of improvements. There was no public participation in or control over the actions of the group — with a situation of this nature such control would have been difficult. The men involved acted as private individuals. There was no central organization that could have been regulated effectively, yet as Baker testified, bad policy could be harmful to the country.

On the other hand, J. P. Morgan and Company and the

National City Bank were performing many of the central banking functions that the nation required but had never authorized. As in 1907, the group organized the reserves of the
financial community and aided solvent banks that were short
of cash. To some degree the group policed the otherwise un-
regulated security markets, attacking the forces of fraud and
corruption. Their policies helped to develop confidence that a
company financed by these leading institutions would be hon-
estly managed in the interest of the security holders, and
thereby probably brought more investors into the public-
security markets.

THE FEDERAL RESERVE ACT

The death of J. Pierpont Morgan in Rome in the spring of
1913 and the passage of the Federal Reserve Act in December
of the same year mark the end of the period in which the
"money trust" exercised its greatest influence. Ever since the
depression of the nineties and particularly since the panic of
1907 Republican Congressional leaders had been discussing
plans for a new banking system — one that would create a
more elastic currency and weaken the hold of big New York
banks over the ultimate reserves of cash and specie. Conservatives wanted a privately owned central bank like that of England or France. "The banking interests of the country wanted
a change," wrote Democratic leader Oscar W. Underwood,
"but they wanted the change so made that they might control.
The party in power was politically afraid to give them control
and therefore did nothing." [5] The progressives in both major
parties favored a government-controlled system such as that
operated by the governments of Indiana and Ohio in the early
nineteenth century.

The Democratic bill, pushed through Congress in 1913, was
a compromise, but one that appeared to favor the progressive
view. As a result "the managers of the new federal reserve
banks of the country found that the welcome accorded to them
by the banks of the country was, to say the least, cool." [6]

Rather than establish a single bank in New York, the new

system created twelve Federal Reserve Banks, each owned by the banks of its district. National banks had to subscribe to the stock of their district bank; state banks might join the system by subscribing. The unifying control in the system was the Federal Reserve Board with five members appointed by the President, each from a different district, plus the Comptroller of the Currency and the Secretary of the Treasury. The district banks were controlled by boards of nine members, of which six members, three bankers and three nonbankers, were representatives of the stockholding banks, and three more were appointed by the Federal Reserve Board. Of these last, one was designated as Federal Reserve Agent and Chairman. Presumably the agents would guide the execution of policies decided on by the Federal Reserve Board, but the board of the district bank also elected a governor to be in charge of banking operations.

The Federal Reserve banks did banking business only with members of the system who might rediscount eligible commercial paper, which made up a large part of the holdings of big city banks, in return for Federal Reserve notes. By lowering or raising the interest rate charged for rediscount the Reserve bank could encourage or discourage borrowing by member banks. Since the Reserve banks were limited to 6 per cent return on their stock, they would presumably use their power over rates with a view to market stability rather than profit. The central board also could step in and control rediscount rates.

In addition to attempting to control the volume of bank credit by manipulating the rediscount rate, the Reserve banks might buy and sell government securities. Selling took cash from the money market and added to the reserves of the district bank; buying had the reverse effect. After 1916 the Reserve banks might also advance money to members on government securities.

In theory the power of government through the central board and their appointees on the district boards seemed so great that bankers feared the system, and state banks generally refused to join. In practice, however, the local governors, the men actually in charge, soon assumed the leadership. Until 1929, Benjamin Strong, as governor of the Federal Reserve Bank of New York, was the most important figure in the system. By thus relegating the Federal Reserve Board and its agents to a secondary position, the leaders of the New York money market continued to exercise much of their old power.

Commenting on the role of the Federal Reserve System in the runaway stock-market boom, Winthrop D. Aldrich of Chase National Bank testified: "The rediscount rate of the New York Reserve Bank remained unchanged from July 13, 1928 to August 9, 1929 . . . This long postponement , , , has come to be regarded as quite the most conspicuous failure of the Federal Reserve System since its inception." [7]

### ORGANIZED FINANCE AND WORLD WAR I

While the Federal Reserve System gave member banks a source of emergency cash that was not controlled by the leaders of Wall Street, it did not directly affect the activity of the big investment banking houses. And, in spite of the fact that the younger J. P. Morgan lacked the Napoleonic qualities of old Pierpont, the trend of events increased for a time the power and prestige of the House.

World War I began in Europe during a deepening depression in the United States. In 1914 the nation was a net debtor on the balance of international security holdings to the extent of about two and a half billion dollars. With the likelihood of war many Europeans temporarily preferred cash to securities and tried to sell on the American market. So heavy were the selling orders on Monday, July 31st, at a few minutes before ten in the morning, that according to the President of the New York Stock Exchange, "A half-hour's session . . . would have brought on a complete collapse; a general insolvency in brokerage houses would have forced the suspension of all business . . . It is idle to speculate what the final outcome might have been." [8] The Board of Governors voted not to open the Exchange. Other exchanges took similar action, and unrestricted trading in stocks was not resumed until April 1915.

Instead of producing a flood of orders, the first effect of World War I was to cut the demand for American goods. Civilian orders dropped, and the governments of both sides regarded their supplies of matériel as sufficient. To prevent drains on the American gold supply, the House of Morgan organized the leading bankers in a pool to limit the export of gold. Not until the spring of 1915 did European orders begin to come in sufficient volume to relieve the depression and reverse the flow of money.

The Allies foresaw the ultimate need for credit in the American market and at once approached the House of Morgan for a loan. Somewhat reluctantly the American House took the matter up with the State Department, with the result that President Wilson on August 15, 1914, made a statement against any loans to belligerent nations. As the needs of the Allies became more pressing, Robert Lansing, the legal counselor of the State Department, opposed Secretary of State Bryan's strict ideas regarding financial neutrality. In October 1914, Lansing persuaded Wilson to issue a statement that short-term bank credits for facilitating trade were not to be subject to the ban on loans. Since such notes were sold by the seaboard banks as acceptances (paper endorsed by a bank) to banks in the interior, and renewed when the notes came due, the distinction between credits and loans was tenuous.

The managing of a vast amount of ninety-day credit which was in fact not self-liquidating became increasingly awkward. Following the resignation of Bryan over the severe presidential attitude toward Germany in the Lusitania sinking of May 1915, the New York banking leaders pressed for government approval of allied loans. Lansing, who had become Secretary of State, urged this policy on Wilson and, in September of 1915, the President relaxed his opposition.

J. P. Morgan and Company now undertook the syndicate leadership for a $500,000,000 Anglo-French loan. The leaders had unusual difficulty in placing the loan. The general attitude on the part of the public that was pro-Ally appeared to be one of supreme confidence in the ultimate victory of their side. They felt no great pressure to buy bonds. In marketing this and subsequent Allied loans, the House of Morgan became a major factor in sustaining the Allied cause, and added still more to its enormous prestige as the leader of Wall Street.

By 1917 Allied credit was breaking under the strain of what then seemed massive creation of international debt. Some $2,000,000,000 in bonds and $1,000,000,000 in theoretically short-term paper had been absorbed by the American market, and the financial houses doubted their ability to market large additional issues. It was at this juncture that Germany solved the problem by bringing the United States government to the assistance of the Allies.

It might have been difficult to keep the United States out of war. The country was deeply involved economically with the success of the Allied cause, and continued prosperity depended on the sale of supplies to Britain and France. The House of Morgan had been the leader in financing the Allies, and neither it nor many other important American firms were neutral in attitude. It seems almost certain that Wilson's neutrality would not have stretched to the point of standing aside from an allied defeat. But when all of this has been said, the fact still remains that Germany deliberately took the risk of war with the United States by resuming unlimited submarine warfare in February 1917. Wilson had now merely to implement his previously announced policy of arming American merchant vessels, and war inevitably followed.

Liberty loans by the government removed the pressure from the banking community, but also made the leading investment houses less important both in the war effort and in the postwar market. By 1920, twenty-one billion dollars' worth of government bonds made all previous bond selling efforts appear insignificant. Furthermore the easy money market created by this enormous base for additional credit plus high income and savings undermined the controlling position of the members of the former "money trust." In the money market of the twenties, syndicates of relatively obscure or new houses could handle hundred-million-dollar issues without recourse to the old financial leaders.

A DECADE OF OVERCONFIDENCE

Although their influence over new issues had declined, the older and larger houses cannot be absolved from whatever blame attaches to being caught in the general wave of over-optimism of the late twenties. While issues sponsored by the House of Morgan, for example, stood up better and had fewer defaults in the thirties than the average of those marketed by others, nevertheless the Morgan name was attached to some of the vulnerable holding company issues, and Morgan credit supported unwise financial operations such as those of the Van Schweringens. The record of the National City and First National Banks and their security selling affiliates, which had been formed before the war, was much the same.

By 1928 Wall Street came to believe that the old-fashioned business cycle had been eliminated. "With the assistance of the Federal Reserve System," wrote Paul M. Mazur of Lehman Brothers, "we may expect freedom from the unwarranted and annoying financial panics of the past . . ." [9] All but a handful of financiers were won over to the speculative enthusiasm. "There was a great deal of atmosphere," recollected President Albert H. Wiggins of the Chase Bank.[10]

The twenties had opened inauspiciously with a deep depression in 1921 and early 1922, but in 1923 business boomed and except for brief recessions in 1924 and 1927 prosperity continued until the last two months of 1929. While investment in real capital goods proceeded at a moderate pace, the war bonds and the increasing willingness of banks to lend money with common stocks as security produced a mounting credit inflation, mirrored in soaring urban real-estate and stock-market prices.

The easy money market tempted all types of operators, from the main street office building promoter to the utility holding company tycoon, to think up new schemes for marketing securities. Big mortgages, often based on optimistic estimates of the value of hotels or office buildings, were broken up into five-hundred or thousand-dollar units and sold to small investors. The readiness of the public to buy the stock and bonds of pyramided holding companies made it possible for a few utility magnates like Samuel Insull or S. Z. Mitchell to control operating properties worth hundreds of millions with a negligible investment of their own.

Elaborate pyramids were chiefly confined to the railroad and public-utility industries where investors had faith in the ultimate earning power of the operating units.[11] In manufacturing one or two levels of holding companies were frequently used as an ownership or managerial convenience, but seldom as a device for drawing in more capital. The arguments advanced for the elaborate pyramid was that managerial and operating efficiency was promoted by bringing companies together. In some instances where public-utility lines crossed and interwove, or railroads duplicated facilities, the argument seemed sound, but where the operating companies were remote from each other the economies were trifling. Often the over-all result was more managerial expense rather than less.

The role of the holding company in the boom of the twenties, however, was dependent not upon its efficiency or inefficiency, but upon the popularity of its stock as a speculative security. Mid-West Utilities, Electric Bond and Share, and other similar stocks soared to heights that bore no relation to the earnings of the operating companies. And at these inflated values the stocks were used as security for loans with the proceeds of which other properties were purchased. When prices crashed in the thirties, the Insull pyramid was found to be an incredibly tangled mass of intercompany obligations, a family tree in which children came to control their parents, and brothers and sisters lived by borrowing from each other.

Another of the devices that flourished in the easy money market was the investment trust. The investor with small savings could not directly achieve the security that comes from diversification of holdings, but he could accomplish this by buying a few shares in the trust, which would invest in a wide range of securities. By 1929 there were nearly four hundred investment trusts.

As in the case of the pyramided holding company, there was nothing wrong in principle in such an arrangement; the trouble came from speculative and unwise use of the funds. Instead of making diversified purchases as disinterested investors, the officers of the trust often bought large blocks of stock in order to gain control of companies, in effect perverting their trusteeship for personal power. Later, some trusts were used as dumping grounds for large blocks of stock that insiders wished to dispose of. The Senate Committee investigating stock-exchange practices saw the investment trust as "the vehicle employed by individuals to enhance their personal fortunes in violation of their trusteeship, to the financial detriment of the public." [12] As a result, the stocks of investment trusts declined more during the depression than the average of the market as a whole.

Meanwhile the character of American banking was changing to fit the new relationships of credit, saving, and investment. With good rates of profit and a slackening in the rate of real capital expansion (see p. 25), successful companies found themselves relatively independent of banks. Before 1914 many companies had used most of their savings for expansion and provided for working capital, and even some fixed capital, by bank loans. In the twenties they tended to retire such loans from profits, and if additional capital was needed, to turn to the security market rather than the banks. Commercial banks, therefore, did less lending on sixty- or ninety-day renewable paper or open credit lines. When big businesses came to banks for money, they were likely to offer stocks and bonds as securities for sizable loans. This gave the banks less paper than could be rediscounted, and so reduced the ability of the Federal Reserve System to control the money market through manipulating the rediscount rate. The change also produced large loans secured by thousands of shares of common stock which could not be sold readily on a declining market.

The urban real-estate and stock-market booms brought prosperity to the metropolitan banks, and the larger ones grew still larger through mergers. But in many country districts land values declined and small local banks, unable to collect their loans, failed by the hundreds: nearly a thousand went down in the prosperous year of 1926. As a result of mergers and failures, the total of nearly 31,000 banks in 1920 had fallen to 25,000 by 1929.

The stock-market boom that followed the mild recession of 1927 and ended in the crash of 1929 must be seen in the light of the new financial arrangements. In spite of agricultural depression, a tapering-off of the market for most forms of capital goods, and no general increase in salaries or wages, the financial mechanisms created a runaway bull market.

To some extent this market was a product of salesmanship. Charles E. Mitchell, Chairman of National City Bank, trained young men and women to sell securities and then sent them out to find the investors. They and their counterparts from other leading banking and brokerage houses rang the doorbells of prosperous-looking citizens and urged them to increase their commitments in order to share in the speculative gains. Margin accounts were carried legally with as little as 25 per cent equity, and temporarily with much less; homes and businesses were mortgaged to buy common stocks; and with this inflow of money the market rose higher and higher without regard to underlying economic probabilities.

In the scramble to make money by selling securities the old leaders of Wall Street were as culpable as the new. National City, Chase, and First National Banks through their security affiliates and Lee, Higginson, Kidder, Peabody, and the House of Morgan all marketed securities of questionable worth to gullible customers. As A. H. Wiggins explained, it was "the times."

The widespread frenzy for easy profits literally pulled itself along by its own bootstraps. Buying on installment or by discounting stock-market profits through increasing loans produced record-breaking consumer purchases in 1929. Employment in finance rose to a point where the salaries and wages of such workers exceeded those in mining and agriculture combined. But such a process had its limits. Customers became loaded with installments, the effective demands for housing and luxuries were temporarily met, and the fact that capital-goods investment was not proceeding rapidly threatened employment.

At all events — and the precise relationships in the boom and collapse of 1929 are still the subject of intensive study — the more cautious Wall Street operators, noting the decline of automobile sales and new housing, began to doubt the stability of high security prices by the late summer of 1929. In spite of withdrawal by such cautious insiders, and contracting broker's loans, stock prices advanced into September and maintained high levels until October. People who had come to depend on stock market profits for their new clothes or automobiles could not afford to withdraw from the market. By October 1, 1929, the value of listed stocks on the New York Stock Exchange, which had been $27 billion on January 1, 1925, stood at $87 billion.

The collapse of the speculative structure came in a series of breaks, that started on October 15, of which the most serious was that of Thursday, October 24, when nearly thirteen million shares were traded, and prices underwent the greatest decline in the history of the stock exchange. Some issues dropped many points before any bid was forthcoming. And brokers frequently sold the stocks of their margin accounts without giving the "owner" time to supply more cash.

At this juncture the partners of the House of Morgan tried to stem the panic as J. Pierpont had in 1907. Early in the day leading bankers met conspicuously at 23 Wall Street, the Morgan "Corner," and early in the afternoon partner Thomas W. Lamont announced that they would support the market. Later, Richard Whitney, representing the House of Morgan on the floor of the exchange, walked to the post where United States Steel was selling for 190, and dramatically bid 205 for 25,000 shares. But all such efforts did not greatly exceed the success of King Canute with the waters of the sea. The pressure for liquidation was too strong to be arrested by Wall Street leadership.

In 1907 the greatest service of J. Pierpont Morgan and his associates had been in saving banks from failure as the results of runs. In the successive market breaks of October, November, and December 1929, the failure of metropolitan banks was not a serious issue. For the time being the Federal Reserve System cushioned the shock and the depositors were not panicky. For these reasons it was possible for President Hoover to call it a speculative panic and to reassure the public that the sound productive processes of the country had not been impaired.

### WHAT WAS "FINANCE CAPITALISM?"

The collapse of 1929 marked the end of a period in United States history during which investment bankers had exerted unusual influence in the economy. From their rise to power in the eighties and nineties, investment houses had become increasingly interested in the financial management of highly capitalized companies. J. P. Morgan and Company and its Wall Street allies symbolized, and to a degree led, the movement. Although business power is a vague concept, it seems safe to say that during the first thirty years of the twentieth century the House of Morgan was the most influential American firm.

But how influential was any single business firm in a group of hundreds of big companies and thousands of medium size? The direct Morgan influence was chiefly in finance, railroads, shipping, electricity, and large-scale manufacturing. Up to the 1920's, at least, the influence of other Wall Street houses was generally confined to the same areas. The new automobile industry and the old textile industry were conspicuous examples of scores of types of business in which investment-banking influence in the first two decades was slight. In small-scale manufacturing, wholesaling, retailing, and service, which comprised most of American business activity, there was no discernible period of finance capitalism. That in times of crisis, such as 1907, 1914, 1921, or 1929, the "money trust" seemed to be at the helm of the economic ship may have been because the disturbances were of a financial nature, and the financiers were at the scene of action.

The stock-market boom of the late twenties appears in

retrospect to have been a time when the people of the country temporarily lost their sane judgment. But how many people? Perhaps four million out of nearly fifty million people with incomes had any stock-market holdings, and there were only half a million margin accounts. To control such a small group in the interests of national stability would seem an obvious solution, but unfortunately the small group were the most influential citizens, not only in finance, but also in industry, trade, and politics.

In the middle of this period of the increasing influence of financiers the country acquired a banking system designed to break the control of Wall Street over ultimate bank reserves and to provide a more elastic currency and credit. The Federal Reserve system partly achieved these purposes. It might also have produced greater financial stability if problems had been visualized in advance, or the deflationary views of the central board had been more acceptable to the political and business communities. But it took the final lesson of 1929 to bring more adequate powers to the Federal Reserve System, and to produce laws regulating security operations.

In the light of earlier history, perhaps no amount of Federal Reserve action could have prevented some break and ensuing depression. American business had never made the transition from a period of high optimism to one of caution or pessimism without severe financial difficulties. Basic to the situation was a declining rate of real capital formation that was undermining the stock-market boom, and no plans for new major areas of investment appeared in 1929 to alter the trend.

### THE PASSING OF THE OLD ORDER

The cataclysm of 1929 did more than ruin the reputation of financiers; it undermined public faith in the basic philosophy of American business. The business leaders of the late twenties believed in the nineteenth-century idea of a self-regulating capitalist economy based on natural economic laws. The theory called for a society in which government limited its functions to those necessary for physical and legal security;

it assumed that natural laws operated in such a way that the able man who worked hard would benefit society and be financially rewarded; it regarded business depressions "as passing interruptions of progress." [13] Influenced by these beliefs, neither political party held the federal government responsible for unemployment relief or support of the aged. The prevailing philosophy of both major parties in the twenties was unchanged from that expressed in Cleveland's Second Inaugural Address: "While the people should cheerfully and patriotically support their government its functions do not include the support of the people." [14] Pursuing the idea of a limited government, the Republicans held both federal employment and expenditures roughly constant from 1923 through 1929.

Compared with later decades, the old order was an economy of lower wages for workers and higher incomes for the middle and upper classes. According to rough estimates, the share of the national income received by the top 10 per cent had been increasing since at least 1910 and reached nearly 40 per cent of the total by 1929, while that of the lowest 10 per cent had been falling.

In the late twenties the belief that any man could succeed by intelligence and hard work had been given additional force by the stock-market boom. Now it seemed every man could become financially secure by modest saving and investment. John J. Raskob, chairman of the Board of General Motors, and also of the Democratic National Committee in 1928, wrote in the summer of 1929: "If a man saves $15 a week, and invests in good common stocks and allows the dividends and rights to accumulate, at the end of twenty years he will have at least $80,000 and an income from investments of $400 a month. He will be rich. And because income can do that, I am firm in my belief that anyone not only can be rich, but ought to be rich." [15]

The ensuing depression that erased some common stocks altogether and left other speculative favorites at 4 or 5 per cent of their former value, abruptly ended the era that inspired Mr. Raskob's soliloquy. But basic social change is seldom as sudden as it appears to be on the surface of events.

The wholly self-regulating economy and the wholly self-reliant individual had been a myth born of wishing. Although government activities had reached low points at various times in the nineteenth century the states had never completely refrained from regulating and assisting business or owning enterprises. Effective federal regulation of railroads, prepared foods, and drugs had appeared in the first decade of the twentieth century. During the period that federal expenditure was being held down by Coolidge and the Republican Congressional majority, state and local expenditures for paving, public buildings, and other improvements were skyrocketing. The automobile era needed far more public equipment than did the railroad age.

Airplanes and electricity joined the automobile in calling forth both federal and state regulation and support. Airlines and interstate transmission of electric power soon came under federal regulation. Large airports, and the system of beacons to guide flights were publicly owned. Highways and bridges, destined to be the biggest single type of investment other than building construction, fell into the hands of government without protest from private enterprise.

In a long view of United States economic growth, the period of relatively uncontrolled industrial business may be seen as coming to a gradual end between 1870 and 1935 and the aphorisms of the twenties may be heard as parts of a swan song.

# Part Two
## 1930–1955

# 6

## Business in Stagnation and Boom

In no previous period had the American economy swung so violently from prosperity to deep depression and back again as it did in the years 1929 to 1955. The shifts were so violent that they deeply affected not only business but the national culture as well. The United States of the early thirties, with a quarter of its workers unemployed, its business leaders in despair, and its intellectuals thinking in terms of fundamental political and social change, was very different from the self-satisfied nation of the late twenties, or the new government-underwritten society of the forties or fifties.

In viewing the performance of the economy, with the graphic profiles of dollar volume of business, employment, or stock prices suggesting the ups and downs of a roller coaster, a prime question is bound to be, why did it happen this way? Why in a relatively mature and stable society should real national income, after having been nearly cut in half in only three years, treble within the next generation? Businessmen, of course, made the decisions that accounted for these swings, but the decisions were influenced by underlying forces that no one thoroughly understood. Political and social innovations, fathered by depression, were passed on to a period of war and prosperity where they took on new meanings and gave a new form to American society.

### THE ROLE OF TECHNOLOGY

Marked differences in the rate of technological change could explain uneven business performance. Was the period 1925 to 1940 one in which technological change failed to produce new incentives for capital investment by business, and was the period 1940 to 1955 one in which technology encouraged the rapid creation of new capital goods?

The answers to such questions must take into account factors outside the realms of either business or invention. Technological developments such as rural electric power, new high-speed highways for automobiles, or facilities for commercial aviation might have been pushed by both private business and government to a greater extent than they were in the thirties had it not been for the prevailing national psychology. But the element that finally turned the tide and kept it flowing in one direction was technology for war. The highly mechanized and scientific character of modern armament gave a boost to investment in capital goods and demanded complex equipment unprecedented in American experience. Furthermore, even in time of peace the new airborne, electronic, and nuclear equipment was made obsolete by subsequent technological advance at a rate never dreamed of by the automobile or radio industries. In 1954, in a period of as secure a peace as the world appeared likely to enjoy in the foreseeable future, the United States government let thirty-nine billion dollars' worth of contracts for new equipment. In 1932 the entire national income in equivalent dollars had been some ninety billion.

Thus, in a broad sense, the change came from new technology, but more narrowly it resulted from the fact that new devices were needed for war. Had peace continued in the early forties there would seem to be no reason to suppose that the demand for electronic devices, new airports and planes, or atomic-energy plants would have been such as to raise the economy to new heights of productivity.

In the long run, more important than the demands of military technology itself was the stimulation it gave to all forms of industrial reseach. By the 1950's management was "research-minded." Whereas in earlier years research expenditures had often been hard to justify to bankers or boards of directors, now research came to be regarded as the most promising form of investment. By the middle fifties 3,000 companies had research facilities employing 500,000 workers.[1] From the efforts of these workers, carefully oriented toward marketable products or improvements, came an unprecedented demand for new capital investment.

Whether basic science would progress rapidly enough to open new areas when old ones reached stability remained a question. In general, business money was not directly spent on basic scientific experimentation from which wholly new lines of procedure might emerge, but in perfecting and protecting existing processes and ways of doing things, or in a search for improvements which would soon be salable. There were of course exceptions, such as chemical companies' interest in basically new products even if development costs were high, but the tendency was to work for the ultimate refinement of existing equipment or methods. Automobile companies, for example, wanted better performance from gasoline-driven vehicles, not a substitute for the automobile.

From corporate research came great changes in electricity, chemicals, and synthetic materials. Scarcely a major area of American life escaped the effects of these changes. The character of factories, business offices, homes, communications, and transportation was altered. These changes would have insured a certain volume of new investment regardless of the technology of war, but whether it would have become sufficient to produce full employment in the face of continuous technological elimination of jobs remains unanswered.

Many of the new devices displaced workers. Mechanical operations gave way to electrochemical processes that saved labor and were more reliable. As natural products were replaced or modified by synthetic substitutes, there was usually a saving in labor cost.

Such synthetics advanced on a broad front. By 1955 rugs of tufted acetate fiber began to replace the wool carpet of 1930;

other chemical fibers were displacing both cotton and wool in clothing; natural rubber was modified to give it many different qualities; plastics, treated plywood, and synthetic fireproof boards were substituted for wood; and the chemistry of metals became ever more complex.

Such changes meant that, on the one hand, nearly every factory and home operated with less manual work, but, on the other hand, a rapidly expanding chemical industry opened new areas for investment and jobs. To the consumer, the synthetic fibers used in many articles of clothing were the most obvious of the new products. The Du Pont company took the lead in this development. By 1935, after two decades of improvements on the original English and French processes, rayon had gained 80 per cent of the market previously held by natural silks and was making large inroads on the cotton business. Rayon in sheet form made cellophane an airtight wrapping material. Du Pont experiments with synthetic fibers in the late thirties and forties produced Nylon, Orlon, Dacron, and other patented products. The expiration of the Nylon patent in 1955 led to its production by a number of firms. While these developments nearly eliminated raw-silk imports from Japan and threatened the use of wool, some of the chemical processes consumed cotton and other crops such as soy beans that could be grown on cotton land.

Synthetic fibers were separated more by use than by chemical nature from plastics. In the 1860's English and French chemists had developed high-cost plastics, but an American, John Hyatt, first produced a cheap plastic, celluloid, in 1869. This had considerable success as a substitute for ivory in billiard balls and toilet articles, and for linen or cotton in men's collars. Another plastic, bakelite, was used for electrical insulation and for some consumer goods in the early twentieth century. The major upswing in plastics, however, occurred after 1930 when synthetic resins and other foreign inventions were put into production in the United States. By the end of World War II general plastics were nearly as widespread as synthetic fibers.

From the standpoint of massive achievement and demand

for new capital investment, the most important single area of chemical alteration of natural products was in petroleum. Various fractions of crude petroleum became the raw material for a large part of the chemical industry, and chemical advances such as catalytic cracking completely altered oil refining. Although listed separately from the chemical industry by the census bureau, the high-octane gasoline that led, in turn, to high-horsepower gasoline motors was the product of complex chemical processes.

The elimination of manual operations took many forms. Processes controlled by central panels of electrically operated valves and meters were a step toward the automatic factory. Almost every new electrical or chemical process required fewer workers and allowed for more efficient operation than did older methods. Many of the new communication devices within the plant depended on the electronic tube developed before World War I. Operations involving sorting, counting, starting, or stopping were made automatic by the photoelectric cell, and cutting operations were replaced by stamping and pressing. In construction, labor-saving electric welding appeared, and prefabricated synthetic panels began to reduce the need for masons, carpenters, and plasterers. In transportation the steam locomotive was rapidly replaced after 1945 by the Diesel engine, which applied its power through electric motors. Atomic-energy development, relying heavily on electrical processes, promised electric public-utility plants at large savings in man-hours. Pipelines and conveyor belts, old in principle, were greatly extended in the forties and fifties to reduce human handling of materials.

After 1940, the nation did not have to worry about "technological unemployment." War and postwar developments made scarcity of workers and materials a more continuous problem. But the old questions of balance between technological displacement of labor and the expansion of productive equipment that would employ labor always remained.

Apart from its effects on the economy, industrial (as well as government and academic) research made the United States less dependent on England or the rest of Europe for scientific knowledge and new processes. In fact, by the 1940's the United States was abreast of or leading the other nations of the western world in most areas of applied science. After World War II the traditional pattern was noticeably reversed: instead of Americans going to Europe to see what was new, European business leaders sent observers to the United States. And if it used its income wisely, the United States could afford to buy enough research time to maintain its position.

## THE ECONOMIC BACKGROUND

Obviously, over-all figures on economic growth for this period must obscure the character of the business changes. Yet business development after World War II has to be seen in the light of the dramatically altered economic situation. By taking the average figures from a number of different economic statistics for three three-year periods (1928–1930, 1938–1940, and 1948–1950), it is possible to see how the stagnation of the earlier years contrasted with the great upswing of the forties. For example, taking the per capita income, adjusted for changes in price, as a measure of growth, the rate for the earlier period was only 5 per cent, the smallest increase for any like period in American history for which reliable figures have been collected.[2] In fact, the average real per capita income for the decade of the thirties was less than for the twenties.[3] Again, this was something new in reliably measured American experience. In contrast, the averages for the years 1938–1940 and 1948–1950 show that between the two periods real per capita income rose more than 37 per cent, an increase recalling the best decades of the nineteenth century.[4] Furthermore, the same trend continued, with some minor ups and downs, through 1955.

Similar changes were reflected in capital investment. From 1930 to 1939 net capital formation was less than 1 per cent of national income, and in the worst years of the depression the economy as a whole lived on its capital. For 1948 to 1950 the percentage of income going into capital has been estimated at 11.1 per cent, a rate slightly above that of the 1920's, but slightly less than for earlier periods. It should also be noted that the rate of investment, unlike that in the twenties, exceeded the rate of savings by perhaps 1 per cent and therefore had an inflationary effect on prices.[5]

Government underwriting of risk was an important element in maintaining the level of investment. Building construction, the old standby of American capital creation, had been somewhat stimulated by federal mortgage guarantees and slum-clearance expenditures in the late thirties, but the continuing effect of these policies from 1945 on became a major element in the postwar boom. Government-guaranteed mortgages allowed construction firms, responding to the opportunities opened up by prosperity and the automobile, to build vast suburban developments and sell them to customers with little or no down payment.

If one turns from income and investment to physical production, the same patterns of stagnation and boom emerge. From the average for 1928–1930 to that for 1938–1940, physical production of goods lagged slightly behind growth in population. From 1938–1940 to 1948–1950 the average per capita product increased nearly 50 per cent.[6]

In the period 1900–1930 people employed in transportation, public utilities, trade, and finance, who for simplicity have been referred to as those in service, increased much more rapidly than workers in manufacturing (see p. 25). But in the most recent period both depression and military expenditure appear to have halted the trend. The table shows the major changes in general types of employment.

Average Distribution of Employed (in millions) [a]

| Period | Agriculture | Manufacturing | Contract construction | Service | Gov't. (except military) |
|--------|------|------|------|------|------|
| 1928–1930 | 11.3 | 9.9 | 1.5 | 14.5 | 3.0 |
| 1938–1940 | 11.7 | 10.1 | 1.2 | 14.3 | 4.0 |
| 1948–1950 | 10.8 | 14.8 | 2.2 | 20.1 | 5.8 |

[a] Source: Estimates based on samples taken by Bureau of Labor Statistics.

Modern military needs, aside from maintenance of troops, put an emphasis on the manufacture of costly and intricate equipment, but outside of government employment they created little demand for service. The rise of employment in contract construction was to some extent the result of military needs, but even more attributable to government guarantee of mortgages. It is interesting to note that World War II and its aftermath made a larger lasting addition to government civilian employment than did the depression and the New Deal.

Another occupational change was the increasing employment of women. In 1900, employed women accounted for about 13 per cent of the female population, and employed men, 60 per cent of the male. By 1940 the rate had gradually climbed to 20 per cent for women, while the male rate remained relatively constant. The percentages for both sexes jumped during the war, but the employment of males rapidly returned to about 60 per cent, and the rate for women leveled off at around 25 per cent. The approximate doubling of female employment marks both the large increase in office work of all kinds and the replacement of men by women in such jobs. So massive were these shifts that they made the decline of textile factory work and domestic service for women appear small by comparison.

A new aspect of the upswing from 1940 on was the extent to which wage earners benefited. In earlier times wages had usually fallen behind prices during periods of inflation and had risen in purchasing power during the periods of declining prices. Or in economists' terms, wages had tended to be stickier than prices. For a number of reasons, including steady employment, a friendly government, the attitudes of professional management, and strong union organization, wages now outran price increases. Real wages, which had risen slightly in the decade of the thirties, had advanced nearly 40 per cent by 1950. Manual workers were unquestionably better off than ever before in American history and were receiving a larger share of the total national income.

If income after taxes is considered, the change of the forties is even more striking. The average worker with a family of three dependents paid relatively little in taxes, probably no more than 5 per cent of his total income, while the top income receivers, the roughly 1 per cent whose incomes were $15,000 a year or more, paid from 20 to a maximum of 91 per cent. "The share of the top one per cent in total income was 19.1 per cent in 1929," writes Arthur Burns, "and 7.7 per cent in 1946 . . . Since the share of this group dropped 11.4 points out of a total possible drop of 18.1 points, on the basis of this yardstick the country had traveled almost two-thirds of the distance toward absolute income equality." [7] From 1946 on these income relations changed more slowly, but change continued in the direction of higher real wages. As can be seen from the tax rates, the leveling off of high incomes was in large part the result of transferring money from prosperous individuals to the government.

### THE RIDDLE OF STAGNATION

The statistics tell what happened but not how or why. Except for the height of the stock-market boom the twenties were not superficially different from other prosperous decades in American history, but the depression of the thirties was unprecedented in its severity. According to standard series the dollar volume of business sank from 16 per cent above normal in July 1929 to 49 per cent below normal in July 1932, and the descent describes a fairly straight line between the two poists, save for a slight rise in early 1931.[8] No previous depression, according to the same series, had ever deflated the dollar volume of business by more than 35 per cent, but this drop amounted to 56 per cent. Furthermore, the level of the late twenties was not reached again until 1937. During the thirties economists and businessmen perforce addressed themselves to the question of what had happened to the business system.

Responsible economists and political leaders talked of economic stagnation and the mature economy. The American dream of an ever higher standard of living appeared to have ended. Some thought that Thorstein Veblen had been right: the Captains of Business had strangled the economy.

But businessmen, of course, thought differently. One group who were not economic theorists supported the views of the President. "In the large sense," wrote Herbert Hoover, "the primary cause of the Great Depression was the war of 1914–1918. Without the war there would have been no depression of such dimensions." [9] Very briefly and oversimply, the argument was that the war left the Western world with a burden of debt that could not be borne, as well as with currency problems that were never settled. For some years the situation was nursed along with American loans, but since the United States tariff precluded collection of interest and principal through the essential surplus of imports over exports, a day of reckoning had to come. From a Western-world standpoint the war was unquestionably an upsetting factor of great magnitude; from the standpoint of the domestic affairs of the United States the argument is less convincing. American participation in the war was brief, and even in 1918 the economic drain did not rise above 25 per cent of the national income. It appears doubtful whether this short-term shift to war production, or the building up of what was, in relation to the national income, a moderate debt should have caused such violent movements in the economy a decade later or seriously weakened its ability to recover from depression.

Another argument of businessmen, resting on adverse governmental activity, was the complaint that government regulation had already progressed so far by 1930 that enterprise was discouraged and the self-adjusting character of the economy largely destroyed. This school of critics usually dated the beginning of the difficulties from state railroad legislation in the 1870's, or the federal Interstate Commerce Act of 1887. The Progressive movement, state and federal, added many more laws regulating working conditions, business combinations, railroads, and public utilities. The conservatives' fear of the effect of these laws was similar to that in the New Deal period. Mark Twain wrote in 1907, "Mr. Roosevelt has done what he could to destroy the industries of the country, and they all stand now in a half-wrecked condition and waiting in an ague to see what he will do next." [10] In this same period corporation and graduated personal income taxes had their beginning. Later there was a widespread fear that the necessary growth in federal power during World War I might lead to socialism. While these fears were proved groundless by the postwar political regimes, it was nevertheless true that business was somewhat more regulated than before the war, and considerably more so than in 1900.

Carrying on the same line of reasoning it was argued that "normal" recovery would have started at a rapid rate in August 1932 had investors not been scared by the probable election of a liberal Democratic president in November. "I do not think there is any question," wrote Paul W. Litchfield of Goodyear, "that America would have worked its way out of that depression if the Hoover Administration had remained in office . . . But the new administration which came into power in 1933 had a different idea. It did not talk about hard work, thrift, resourcefulness. The government would fix things." [11] After the election things went from bad to worse, and after the Roosevelt inauguration, new reforms, regulations, and taxes continued to inhibit the risk-taking activity of entrepreneurs and investors.

There was another facet to this "strait-jacket" argument that was not emphasized by big businessmen. The rigidities blamed on government regulations and the discouragement of new enterprise attributed to taxes or controlled rates could also be regarded as unwanted by-products of big business itself. By the 1920's about half of the industrial production of the United States was in the hands of large corporations. In railroads and public utilities the giant company was practically the rule. No matter how carefully they studied management and operation, these big companies could not preserve the flexibility, speed, and daring of smaller business. New risks were assessed from the standpoint of management's fiduciary obligations to thousands of stockholders; changes were slowly and carefully examined in the light of their effect upon a complex organization; markets were well enough controlled as to both price and production to permit delay in the introduction of upsetting innovations. No one has found quantitative measures that could weigh these various deterrents to recovery, but obviously the problem was one involving many forces.

A widely believed explanation for the falling off of the rate of economic advance was found in the closing of the West and the "maturity" of the economy. President Franklin D. Roosevelt and other New Dealers made much of this argument. The buoyancy and drive of the American economy had depended, they claimed, largely on the development of new western lands by farmers or ranchers, and the exploitation of western lumber and mineral resources by private capital. Speaking in San Francisco in 1932, Roosevelt said, "A glance at the situation today only too clearly indicates that equality of opportunity as we have known it no longer exists. Our industrial plant is built; the problem just now is whether under existing conditions it is not overbuilt. Our last frontier has long since been reached, and there is practically no more free land." [12] Many scholars argued that European economy had expanded in the nineteenth century because of the exploitation of the more temperate and habitable areas of new continents, and the chance for further enterprises of this kind had also greatly diminished. Meanwhile, the "mature" industrial nations had built their basic equipment to a stage where little more investment was needed at home. "Our task now," continued Mr. Roosevelt, "is not discovery or exploitation of natural resources, or necessarily producing more goods. It is the soberer, less dramatic business of administering resources and plants, already in hand . . ." [13]

True as the argument may have been from the standpoint of contemporary psychology, it proved false economically and historically. The "maturing," if it existed at all, was obviously connected with a stage of technology, if technological change were in truth progressing at either a constant or accelerating rate the "maturity" could not last. With the overwhelming majority of the people of the world, including many in Europe and the United States, living in essentially pre-industrial conditions, it seemed far too early to talk of lack of rather routine possibilities for further expansion.

The apparent lack of opportunity may have been partly the result of business attitudes toward risk-taking and investment that were maladjusted to the technological level of the economy — that is, to the *kind* of opportunities offered. Social institutions and psychological factors, affect the course of business activity, and the failure to exploit either American or world-wide opportunities to the utmost may have had, as we shall see later, social-psychological causes.

An explanation of the depression that appealed to large numbers of professional economists in the thirties was put forward by the British theorist and statesman, John Maynard Keynes. His hypotheses regarding reasons for "irregular" performance of the economy were the most exciting and important modifications in classic economic theory since its comprehensive exposition by Alfred Marshall in the late nineteenth century. He started from the established fact that national income was chiefly spent on either producer or consumer goods. But he argued that whereas consumer expenditure depended mainly on the size of the national income and the character of its distribution between the poor and the rich, and for all practical calculations varied only as these elements varied, producer goods expenditure, or investment, depended mainly on the state of business sentiment.[14] The next step in Keynes's argument was that the national income could only increase if investment increased, and vice versa — a proposition with which most businessmen would agree. And finally he concluded that "the duty of ordering the current volume of investment cannot safely be left in private hands," [15] left, that is, to "business sentiment."

He deduced a further theorem that was to form an important justification for progressive taxation and government subsidy or aid to low-income groups. He asserted a "fundamental psychological law that men are disposed, as a rule and on the average, to increase their consumption as their income increases, but not as much as the increase in their income." [16] Obvious corollaries of this law were that more even distribution of income would increase consumption, and that depression could be caused by too much of the national income going to wealthy individuals who neither consumed sufficiently nor invested their surplus in activity employing labor.

Applied to the situation of the thirties, the argument ran that bad income distribution had produced oversaving and underinvestment and hence underemployment of resources. Already acted on by practical politicians, Keynes's book gave these ideas the appeal of the fine logical mechanisms of classic economic theory. Regardless of the truth of the theory, and many disagreed with it as stated by Keynes, it seemed to fit snugly with the American data. As noted in Chapter 2, the share of the top tenth of income receivers had probably been increasing since, at least, 1910. Simon Kuznets' figures, prepared for the National Bureau of Economic Research indicate that the share of the 1 per cent who received the highest incomes increased over 13 per cent between 1919 and 1929.[17] Since practically all of the net saving available for risk-taking investment was made by the top tenth and most of it by the top twentieth,[18] this shift in income distribution could allow a great increase in saving with no proportionate increase in consumption. According to Harold Moulton of the Brookings Institution: "If, in consequence of wide variations in the distribution of income, the proportion of the national income that is saved expands rapidly there results a maladjustment which retards rather than promotes the expansion of capital." [19] With consumption staying nearly the same, the investor might see no available use for his money.

Although the New Dealers and other Western political leaders, who were learning by practice that government spending could create prosperity — the lesson that introduced a new economic era — were happy to embrace Keynes as their prophet, it is not clear that bad income distribution was the chief villain of the early thirties. Figures are lacking for 1900, but it appears likely that concentration of income in the upper brackets was also proceeding during the more satisfactory period of economic growth from 1900 to 1913. One differentiating factor was a rapid rise in agricultural income during the earlier period, as compared with a general tendency to decline from 1920 to 1939.[20]

So the argument on the basis of income distribution is inconclusive and brings us back to psychological questions such as how much does the rate of investment depend on obvious business opportunities that require little imagination? Can one treat such relationships in general theoretical terms or is it not necessary to analyze a particular economy, with particular business outlooks and habits, at a particular juncture in both technology and politics? Two famous business-cycle theorists, Count Kondratieff and Joseph Schumpeter, both answered the second question in the affirmative as far as technology is concerned. They held that certain capital-consuming innovations stimulated long uptrends in economic activity, and in the absence of such innovations the rate of increase declined.

A somewhat similar type of argument is based on changes in the birth rate: a falling rate tends toward economic stagnation, and a rising rate produces increasing demand and therefore increased economic activity. Granting that mortality remains constant or declines, the premises are obviously true, but cause and effect are not clear. It is argued that falling economic activity depresses the birth rate, and vice versa. During these years the birth rate lagged slightly behind marked changes in dollar volume of business, and therefore had a reënforcing effect on any continued movement. From 1929 to 1930, for example, the birth rate rose slightly and then started to fall in 1931. Similarly while the depression of 1937 to 1939 reached bottom in 1938, the year of lowest birth rate was 1939. At all events, a general upward swing in the birth rate after 1939 and a downward swing in mortality after 1936 gave added support to the long boom.

Whether or not the failure of American investment in physical equipment to revive automatically after 1929 was caused by the effects of World War I, government regulation, the inflexibility of big business, newly achieved economic maturity, an income distribution that produced "excessive" saving, or the absence of fortuitous innovations requiring large capital investment, the lag in capital formation had become marked even in the late twenties. In 1924 financing that resulted in additions to physical equipment was 76 per cent of the net total of new financing; in 1929 it was only 35 per cent. Furthermore, the dollar total was lower, standing at $3,186,-000,000 in 1929 as against $3,466,000,000 in 1924.[21] Somehow or other, in spite of continuing changes in technology, American productive investment had reached a nearly static level, one too low for the expansion of the economy at its old rate. With the collapse of demand in the depression there was consequently little incentive for investment in new equipment.

### THE GREAT BOOM

The greatest depression in American history may remain the subject of argument for many years, but there is almost no dispute regarding the basic causes of the greatest boom. The demands of war on an unprecedented scale, the entrance of government into both innovation and the encouragement of capital investment, the backlog of normal consumer demand from four years of war, and continuing government expenditure in the postwar years are sufficient causes for the boom, and they collectively were of such magnitude as to be beyond dispute. The rise in government expenditures at all levels from 15 per cent of national income in 1929 to 21 per cent in 1949 has already been noted. From 1950 to 1953 federal expenditures, chiefly for armament and war went up about 90 per cent, and in spite of a simultaneous rise in the national income of nearly 50 per cent (roughly from 200 to 300 billion), the percentage of the total national income going to the government mounted to 28 per cent. Or, to put it another way, well over a quarter of the value of the nation's economic transactions depended on the government.

There were in addition many other factors to which the exponents of different ideologies attached varying degrees of importance. During the period after 1940, for example, government activities were generally of a type that encouraged risk by the investor and the entrepreneur. And the atmosphere of government under Truman and Eisenhower was generally "businesslike" and conservative. In fact by 1943 full employment and prosperity had routed the "liberals" in Congress, and legislation came more and more under the control of "conservative" southern Democrats and Republicans.

Postwar armament expenditures, increasing population, atomic development, Marshall plans for dollar aid to Europe, government-financed housing, and mortgage guarantees all aided business in maintaining a high level of new investment. Probably for the first time since the early years of the century, investment in time of peace was outrunning savings. Hitherto, as in the early 1880's, 1890's, and 1900's, such situations had led to brief inflationary booms followed by panics, but now the continuing demands of the city-to-suburbs movement, the stimulating effects of changes in military technology, and new turns in the "cold war" kept the boom going. Moderate recessions in 1949 and 1954 were apparently cured by the easing of financial controls, promises of lower taxes, and an unbalanced budget. That the stimulating effect of government spending had been learned by both political parties was shown by the Republican refusal in the early years of the Eisenhower administration to balance the budget even in a time of boom prosperity.

Another factor in the great prosperity was more even distribution of income. The most advanced advocates of the general Keynesian formulas of taxing away high savings, offering government incentives to investment, and legislating higher wages in order to increase employment would scarcely have proposed a greater readjustment in the thirties than had taken place by the late forties. By 1952 nearly half the families in the United States had incomes between $3,000 and $6,000, and only about a third had less than $3,000. The fact that investment was outrunning savings, that employment was nearly as full as is likely in a complex economy, and that this situation existed without a speculative boom, left small space, for the moment, for the Keynesian type of criticism. Or perhaps the conditions deduced by Keynes for full employment had been met.

In this new business system consumers were playing a greater part than ever before. In proportion to their incomes they were buying a quarter again as many refrigerators, washing machines, automobiles, and other durable goods as in 1929.[22] And they were also investing a larger part of their income in new homes. From 1946 to 1951 nearly six million dwelling units were built, the great majority for occupancy by their owners.[23] By 1950 half the buildings used for homes were occupied by owners, and 60 per cent of all the durable equipment in the country, which included factories, power plants, railroads, buildings, trucks, automobiles, and similar utilities, was being used directly by consumers for their own purposes.[24]

Gratifying as was the picture of a nation of prosperous property-holders, each with his house, automobile, television set, washing machine, radio, and a dozen other semidurable utilities, the situation introduced a new element of instability in the economy. When the great mass of people had to spend all of their earnings on necessities their demand was predictable on the basis of their income, but in an economy where average income was high enough to allow for discretion in expenditure the relation of income to consumer expenditure in any given period was uncertain. Consumer decisions as to when to buy or not to buy such unnecessary articles as new television sets, fur coats, or automobiles might depend upon their estimates of the future trend of prices just as in the case of business purchases. In Keynesian terms "sentiment" could now rule in consumer expenditures as well as in business investment. The recession of 1949 was deepened by consumer restraint, and the inflationary boom after the outbreak of the Korean war in 1950 was partly the result of consumers' decisions to stock up with durables before rationing was imposed or prices went higher.[25]

The new position of the farmer in the boom of the forties produced a group of discretionary buyers in that previously hard-pressed sector of the economy. Farm purchasing power, besides sharing the general instability connected with luxury durables, also depended on government policies and price supports. Furthermore, farm production was in the hands of fewer and more efficient farmers than in 1930. In that year farm owners and managers were 12 per cent of the labor force, and farm population some 25 per cent of the total. By 1950 the respective figures were 7 per cent and 16 per cent with the trend still downward. This smaller group of more prosperous men would be more likely to fit their purchases to anticipated price movements.

Another unstable element in the postwar prosperity was unbalanced foreign trade. The normal trade of a creditor nation receiving interest on investments abroad should show a surplus of imports. The United States, however, was exporting billions of dollars more in goods than it was importing. Its customers were able to pay for these goods from foreign-aid payments and new loans. If heavy subsidies to foreign nations continued, the export balance could be maintained, but an end to such payments would mean a sharp curtailment of American sales abroad.

The generally high-level prosperity of 1950 to 1955, therefore, was inherently no more stable than that of the late twenties, perhaps less so. To fluctuations produced by the guesses of entrepreneurs, including farmers, had now been added the uncertainties of consumer forecasts. The facts that the major type of investment was in small homes 40 per cent supported by government-guaranteed mortgages, and that a principal type of demand was government purchase of war material might or might not be regarded as stabilizing elements. Both types of government support appeared likely to continue.

The problem for the future seemed to be whether greater knowledge of the interrelations within the economy, a more dynamic technology and more flexible government action would overcome the mounting elements of instability. At least there had been no collapse following World War II, such as that of 1920 and 1921. What would have followed the recessive tendency of 1949 and the recovery of the spring of 1950 was hidden for all time by the Korean war, but a more pronounced recession in 1953 and 1954 was ended by favorable govern-

bol of wealth, was becoming rare; there was no longer a depressed immigrant or agricultural labor group to provide cheap servants, and the mobility of corporate executives was such that they hesitated to invest more in any one location than could be easily recovered through a sale. Sociologist David Riesman wrote on the new trend of the upper group toward "inconspicuous consumption." [8]

Reënforcing these trends was the increasing equality of income after taxes. Taxes appeared destined to remain high and to be progressive against larger incomes on both the state and national levels. Aside from preparation for war, the society needed streets, highways, schools, colleges, hospitals, and other collective facilities on a scale never thought of by earlier generations, and the money, of course, had to come from taxes. During the nearly continuous boom from 1940 on, elastic business expense accounts and tax savings on capital gains did encourage a good deal of lavish consumption, but any prolonged halt in increasing business activity and the rising value of equities would greatly narrow the range of spending.

In the field of social welfare and philanthrophy, bureaucratic action was superseding the individual decisions of successful businessmen. Since the government allowed corporations to contribute a part of their income to charitable or educational institutions before paying taxes, there was a large saving in having such gifts made directly by the companies rather than by the receivers of already taxed dividends. This led to the setting up of general foundations, and to direct corporate support of higher education. Explaining his participation in this movement, Chairman Frank W. Abrams of the Standard Oil Company of New Jersey said, "I know I can't take any credit for this. I'm just an ordinary business guy that got shoved into something. It's like being thrown into a Billy Sunday meeting, I suppose, and getting converted. You didn't want to go in, but somebody pushed you — they thought you needed it. And it has been rather overwhelming, and highly satisfying." [9]

The importance of this shift was probably not in its influence on the character of education or welfare agencies. Some thinkers saw in the trend a danger that higher education, perhaps the most influential conditioning force for the political and social ideas of future leaders, would fall under the control of business, and a few businessmen, by writing of the obligation of the colleges to teach the free-enterprise system, added to these fears; but private education had always been supported by men who had made their money in business. The donors seemed no more likely to interfere with academic freedom as corporate executives than similar men had as private citizens. The real importance of the entrance of the corporation as an entity in the field of giving was the emergence of the big company as a quasi-public institution, with social and political responsibilities. The property of a corporation wth several hundred thousand stockholders was not strictly private property, and its actions were not those of a truly private character. To quote John Jessup again, "The fact is that the corporation promises to become a sort of welfare community. That is the best guarantee that we need not have a national welfare state." He saw the corporation as a fresh source of democracy to fight against the encroachment of centralized government.[10] But this was a very impersonal kind of democracy, the democracy of big units rather than the democracy of individuals. There still existed the problem that had beset the corporate form of organization since its beginnings in the early nineteenth century — the inability to achieve a democratic system of operation within the company.

The spirit of business had always been toward the efficient exercise of authority from the top down. But business was the leading institution in a social system called democracy; to be truly representative it too must be democratic. And democracy works from the bottom up. This means more than equality of opportunity for those qualified to rise, more than democratic manners that allow a worker to call the president by his first name. It means policy formation on a participative basis and an increased willingness on the part of business to study and respond to the problems and values of American society. As Sir George Schuster, a British business leader, put it: "If we try, as many of us do who hold managerial responsibilities, to set out a list of ideals which we are to aim at, or which we think are good for people for whose employment we are responsible, then I think we are doomed to disaster. *We have to work with an intelligent population.*" [11]

⤡ One unmistakable clash between democratic and business traditions had come from business' old assumption that workers were purely "economic men," interested only in material satisfactions. The assumption came under attack as a result of Elton Mayo's study at the Hawthorne plant of General Electric in the late 1920's and his book, *The Human Problems of an Industrial Civilization*.[12] But the results of such advanced thinking were slow to spread. As late as 1952 *Time* ran a special two-page section, "Human Relations: A New Art Brings a Revolution in Industry." One of the illustrative cases concerned a change in the method of pajama-making: "One group was simply told of the change, another was told of the necessity for it and permitted to work out for itself the necessary revisions in quotas and rates. Result: the second group's production quickly passed the old average of 60 hourly units per worker, and reached more than 80. The first group barely exceeded 50 units, and 17 per cent of its members shortly quit." The article ended with a statement from Clarence Francis, Chairman of the Board of General Foods: "It is ironic that Americans — the most advanced people technically, mechanically and industrially — should have waited until a comparatively recent period to inquire into the most promising single source of productivity: namely the human will to work. It is hopeful on the other hand that the search is now underway." [13] Despite many articles and books there still existed in 1955 "a great demand for guidance and enlightenment on the part of ... businessmen, who apparently feel all of a sudden that they are deficient in the practice of human relations." [14] Such a feeling of the need to do something in this area was evidence of the persistence of the problem as well as of some progress.

⤡ One weakness in the search for what creates the will to work was the failure to recognize the wholeness of human personality. The will to work depends not only on good working conditions and respect for the dignity of the worker, but also on the employee's approval of the company, its policies, and its role in society. The talk of businessmen and labor leaders alike was still too much in terms of material wants and satisfactions. Eric Larabee, an editor of *Harper's,* noted at the Corning Glass Works' conference of businessmen and scholars that "there was a tendency on both sides to speak of 'human values' as distinct entities, almost as though they had similar qualities to goods and services." [15] Seldom did business discussion rise to the level of searching for new, positive, nonmaterial values that could make business a world-wide standard-bearer of democracy. Lack of democracy was certainly not a failing peculiar to American business. On the contrary, American business was probably more democratic than business anywhere else in the world. The trouble was that in the course of its growth from small shop to great corporation it failed to embody in its structure and operation some basic ideals of American culture.

Defining specific ideals in a complex culture like that of the United States is a difficult task, avoided by most scholars of a scientific bent, and done only impressionistically by visiting literary men or journalistic pundits. Such playing wth abstractions was clearly not a game for active business leaders. Yet there were some cultural common denominators which few Americans would question; values or ideals that found expression in sayings and beliefs passed on to children by generations of parents and by repetition in millions of schoolbooks.

Some of these, such as the belief that rational effort counts, that change is generally good, that active mastery of a problem rather than fatalistic acceptance is the American way, or that interest in the external world of things is better than inner contemplation, reënforced the attitudes of businessmen (see p. 185). But some other themes that emphasized the American democratic and religious heritage, such as the need for justification of behavior in terms of Christian morality, the strong belief in equality as a law of nature or the "cult of the common man," and the right of every adult to have an equal voice in making decisions affecting the common welfare, often conflicted with business action.[16] These were basic ideals, however, that underlay the operation of most social organizations, of almost all Protestant religions, and of all American governments.

The average businessman, whether of 1850 or 1950, would probably subscribe to such ideals in principle, but he would admit, when pressed on the subject, that often they did not appear immediately applicable in business. Business, he might argue, had to have a system of ideals of its own, such as physical efficiency, substantial rewards for unusual ability, and clear lines of authority based on the sanction of ownership. Insofar as the two systems — social and business — were reconcilable, it was on the basis that business was a special part of the nation's activity which justified its deviations from the precepts of the Bible and the Declaration of Independence by a flood of products that made a better life possible in all other spheres. From the sacrifice of certain ideals on the economic altar came their richer fulfillment in the life of the nation.

This rift between business ideals and those of the common people helps to explain the ambiguous popular attitude toward business leaders. They were respected for their material success, their control over jobs, and their ability to supply capital or credit, but regarded as lacking in the moral and spiritual qualities desired in the top level of national leaders. In American folklore the farmer's values and attitudes were virtues, those of the businessman fostered such vices as covetousness and vanity. The upbringing of the poor country boy was idealized and regarded as a guarantee that, even if he later achieved economic success, his basic ideas would be moral in the Protestant religious sense and would be democratic in the common people's sense.

Businessmen were seriously troubled by public distrust only when it took the form of regulatory legislation. The almost unchallenged position of business executives as decision-makers in their own sphere of action over many generations gave them the feeling that their ideas were right and that the public should conform to them. Businessmen tended to regard other types of leaders as unreliable or incompetent. The motives of politicians were suspect as corrupt and insincere. Professors, ministers, and literary men were held to be impractical and likely to have theories dangerous to social stability.

This anti-intellectual attitude had been strong ever since the later nineteenth century. Merle E. Curti, a leading scholar of American thought, notes that "American respect for business, and the businessman's inadequate appreciation of the intellectual have, by tradition, been pretty generally taken for granted." [17] Thus the businessman was to a degree able to live in his part of the culture by his own precepts, regarding other beliefs as unimportant to the main task at hand, the material improvement of the nation.

The tacit assumption of superior business understanding is illustrated by an interesting example. In 1950 Edward Bernays, one of the most prescient and philosophical of public-relations men, promoter of the concept that public relations was a two-way street down which ideas came from the public to business, nevertheless delivered a speech in Boston on "How American Business Can Sell the American Way of Life to the American People." [18] One wonders if a small voice at the other end of the street replied: "How Can the American People Sell the American Way of Life to Business?" Actually, this example is somewhat unfair both to Bernays and to advanced business thought, but it illustrates the unfortunate if more or less unconscious historic assumption that society should conform to what managers deem best for business.

Often serving as the justification for business dogmatism was the idea that business decisions were unalterably based on the requirements of the market. No doubt in the old days of small business, low mechanization, and weak market controls the businessman struggling for survival in a competitive situation had little leeway. But the big companies of the mid-twentieth century, the ones that set the tone of business thinking, had considerable control over prices in the market. And, as already noted, such companies had already gone far in the support of community services, education, and welfare plans for workers.

The fact remains that the *decisions* to do these good deeds were not generally participated in by their beneficiaries. Aside from dealings with organized labor, there were few democratic procedures in business by which opinion from below could effectively influence the major actions of those on top, or by which changes in policy could be opened to advance discussions. The practical difficulties in the way were great, but if business was to be truly democratic, they had to be overcome.

## THE CHALLENGE TO AMERICAN BUSINESS

The unsolved problem of the relations of the business system to democracy was lifted from the realm of theoretical speculation and placed in the forefront of world affairs by the aftermath of World War II. Americans were forced, perhaps for the first time, to assess their culture for its fitness for survival in a competitive world situation, and for the specific elements on which it could base a claim to world leadership. The American business system was placed in an international spotlight. The United States emerged as the only Western nation strong enough to undertake world leadership, and she led from a position of strength based primarily on the success of her economic system. Thus, for better or for worse, American business had become a key protagonist in the physical struggle with world communism.

The contest, however, was not just a matter of material superiority, and the fight for world influence could not be won by economic means alone. If such were the case, America would triumph, and American businessmen, as the directors of these economic forces, would be the world's natural leaders. But the United States was battling for men's minds, their hopes, aims, and allegiance, and it was increasingly evident that success depended on a spiritual and intellectual appeal rather than on mere respect for economic power. Approval had to be voluntary and could not be commanded. And although America had little difficulty selling the products of her fields and factories overseas, her industrial machinery, agricultural implements, petroleum products, grain and crude cotton, and automotive equipment, she had not yet sold the rest of the world on the virtues of American culture.

Because the contacts of the mass of the people with things American were to such a large extent through businessmen and their products, the representatives of the United States' economic power assumed a significant role in this winning of social approval. Thus the very success of American business placed it in a position for which it never consciously prepared, and for which it was not especially fitted. For this purpose at least two adjustments were required: business must fit physically and economically into a state of military strength; and it must find its particular role in the attitudes and beliefs associated with the American world mission.

American industry, whose strength had so largely given rise to this world mission, found its traditional policies thrown into confusion. Business was swept progressively into a new military order of subsidies to foreign nations, massive government investment, stockpiling of scarce materials, and armament manufacture. Should executives resist the advance of peacetime government foreign-aid and arms expenditures at the risk of turning the world over to fascism or communism, or should they accept the administration program at the risk of never again being free from the need of government aid? For a hundred years American private enterprise had prepared its defense against socialist revolution, but it had given little thought to the danger of simply being absorbed by a "capitalist" state.

True choice was scarcely possible since coöperation with government was the road to profits for the stockholders, and such was the traditional aim of management. For those companies with government contracts, and this included most of the giants, it was clearly advantageous to cultivate close relations with government officials, particularly in the Department of Defense. For this purpose, retired generals, admirals, and high-level civilian officials made valuable business executives. Athough quantitatively the movement was small, it raised fears in some minds of a union of undemocratic forces in business and government, at a time when the need seems to be for business to give assurances in the opposite direction.[19]

The challenge to business to play its necessary role in American intellectual and spiritual world leadership was far more difficult to meet than the adjustment to government contracting. In the confident days of 1900, evolution, Christianity, the Anglo-Saxon character, and the virtues of democracy appeared to promise the eventual world supremacy of the American way. But now the struggle for supremacy was no longer some unforeseeable situation of the future. And much of the spiritual equipment counted on in 1900 was relatively ineffective. The ways of evolution had become a mystery; conventional Christianity, though strong at home, seemed a weak weapon against communism; the strength of Anglo-Saxon character no longer controlled the people of backward areas; and the political institutions of the Ango-American tradition were easily misunderstood and often not immediately applicable to people differently trained.

The one aspect of American life that the whole world continued to respect was its material success. Indeed, the American business system was now the strongest card the United States and her allies held in the contest with world communism. If the rest of the world could be shown that American business principles were an integral part of a larger value system beneficial to them and possibly adoptable, it might be won over.

On balance, the chronicle of the changes in business ideology since 1900 augured well for the future. Business had modified its ideas and adapted itself to the inevitable changes in the social and political complexion of the country. Granted that the adjustments were often made grudgingly and sometimes incompletely, yet they were made. From a philosophy of the self-regulating economy presided over by an elite group who could take care of themselves and who had no responsibility for the welfare of others, businessmen as a whole came to a realization that bigness necessitated certain governmental controls over the economy; they accepted the fact that with their position of great influence in the nation must go some accountability for the general well-being.

Nevertheless, business was far from ready to assume the missionary task which was thrust on it. It had to work at making its own internal operations reflect more adequately the democratic ideals to be communicated abroad. A more basic problem, the same one which confronted all other segments of society, was the need for reanalysis and rearticulation of the ideals and values Americans wanted the rest of the world to accept.

The paradox noted in 1900 still existed in 1950. In spite of the widely held view that the United States was a "business society," the great majority of the people who worked for salaries or wages did not regard themselves as businessmen. Regardless of prosperity, better public relations, and more independent business enterprisers in relation to the rest of the population, a feeling of unity with the aims of business leadership seemed lacking. People apparently respected but did not trust business leaders. Corporations might in truth be becoming guardians of the common welfare, but the public was not yet convinced. In May 1949, according to a Roper poll, "A majority of the people . . . believe that very few businessmen have the good of the nation in mind when they make their important decisions . . . They think, therefore, that government should keep a sharp eye on business." [20] American businessmen, for all their important position in society, did not epitomize America as did the independent farmers of an earlier era.

Probably business could not hope to succeed in any attempt to mirror the total value structure of the society. Yet that did not lessen the need for clarification of the various traditions and beliefs which might be strengthened at home and urged on the rest of the world. Philosophers and anthropologists pointed to the confusion and conflict in American values; writers on religion questioned especially some of business' ethical precepts, asking "whether the secular functions of society, each existing of itself and for itself, can be relied on to serve human destiny." [21]

Much of the conflict, much of the apparent lack of unity and purpose in American national life, came from the failure we have noted to reconcile business attitudes and aims, such as the pursuit of an ever higher standard of living, with the other fundamental values stemming from American religious and democratic traditions. If business could look at itself, analyze its values, and try to realign them with those broader ideals of the good society, it could help to make stronger and more valid America's message to an uncertain world.

Part of the realignment of business attitudes would be good business. At the stage of technology present in mid-century United States, greater productivity resulted from treating the employee as a human being who would be attached to his work by intellectual approval and a sense of "belonging" at the job as well as by the need of the pay check. The managements that adopted the gospel of the democratic custodianship of economic opportunity were going to have improved morale from top to bottom.

Big business was beginning to move in this direction. Small and medium-sized business was still highly competitive, was often inadequately financed, and had less leeway to take non-material considerations into account; here progress would probably be a matter not of years but of decades. From the standpoint of public relations at home, this was discouraging, since most Americans worked for small or medium-sized business. The image of the society presented abroad, however, might change more rapidly. Almost all foreign contacts were with the agencies or products of sizable American companies, organizations large enough at least to be conscious of their place in a new business order and to be capable of providing leadership in that direction if they wanted to.

To hope for moral or spiritual inspiration from any size of business was asking for new functions from an institution originally designed to supply only material wants. But the modern corporation had inevitably become more than an economic institution, and its managers had more than material responsibilities. In the words of Meyer Kestnbaum, President of Hart Shaffner and Marx, "We need now some people to tell us how to convert industrialism, which has great power, into the force for good in our own country and elsewhere that it can be. If we meet that challenge, I will say again that we are on the verge of a golden age." [22]

# ${\mathcal{N}otes}$

CHAPTER 1. BUSINESS AS AN AMERICAN INSTITUTION

1. William Miller, "American Lawyers in Business and Politics," *Yale Law Journal* (January 1951), p. 68n.

2. Henry C. Potter, *The Citizen in His Relation to the Industrial Situation* (New Haven: Yale University Press, 1902), p. 162.

3. André Siegfried, *America Comes of Age* (New York: Harcourt, Brace, 1927), p. 165.

4. F. X. Sutton, S. E. Harris, Carl Kaysen, James Tobin, *The American Business Creed* (Cambridge: Harvard University Press, 1956), p. 23.

5. Ralph Henry Gabriel, *The Course of American Democratic Thought* (New York: Ronald Press, 1940), p. 155.

6. Lewis Atherton, *Main Street on the Middle Border* (Bloomington: University of Indiana Press, 1954), p. 28.

7. Carl Snyder, "American Captains of Industry," *American Monthly Review of Reviews*, XXV (April 1902), 418, 432.

8. Theodore Roosevelt, "Solitude and Longitude Among Reformers," *Century Magazine*, LX (June 1900), 216.

9. Quoted in Allan Nevins, *Ford: The Times, the Man, the Company* (New York: Scribners, 1954), p. 579.

10. Atherton, *Main Street on the Middle Border*, p. 3.

11. *The Autobiography of William Allen White*, pp. 4, 131, 429. See also pp. 51, 62, 98, 101, 114, 179, 187, 219, 244, 325. References as published in the *New Yorker*, April 20, 1946, p. 90.

12. Atherton, *Main Street on the Middle Border*, p. 23.

13. William Miller, "American Historians and the Business Elite," *Journal of Economic History*, IX (November 1945), 204.

14. William Jennings Bryan, Cross of Gold Speech, July 8, 1896, quoted in Henry Steele Commager, ed., *Documents of American History* (New York: Crofts, 1934), p. 175.

15. Quoted in Matthew Josephson, *The President Makers* (New York: Harcourt, Brace, 1940), p. 74.

16. *Ibid.*, p. 86.

17. *Ibid.*, p. 75.

18. Claude G. Bowers, *Beveridge and the Progressive Era* (Boston: Houghton Mifflin, 1932), p. 68.

19. Charles E. Perkins (President, Chicago, Burlington & Quincy Railroad) to Thomas Potter, November 18, 1884, quoted in Thomas C. Cochran, *Railroad Leaders, 1845–1890* (Cambridge: Harvard University Press, 1953), p. 437.


CHAPTER 2. FUNDAMENTALS OF BUSINESS CHANGE

1. Richard J. Walsh, "The Doom of the Self-Made Man," *Century Magazine*, CIX (December 1924), 258, quoted in Irvin G. Wyllie, *The Self-Made Man in America* (New Brunswick: Rutgers University Press, 1954), p. 169.

2. Lewis Mumford, *Technics and Civilization* (New York: Harcourt, Brace, 1934), pp. 151–210.

3. Frederick W. Taylor, *Scientific Management* (New York: Harpers, 1911), pp. 6–7.

4. C. E. Ayres, *Theory of Economic Progress* (Chapel Hill: University of North Carolina Press, 1944), p. 153.

5. *Ibid.*, pp. 119–120.

6. Nevins, *Ford,* p. 348.

7. George V. Thompson, "Intercompany Technical Standardization in the Early Automobile Industry," *Journal of Economic History*, XIV (Winter 1954), 6.

8. Thomas C. Cochran, *The Pabst Brewing Company: The History of an American Business* (New York: New York University Press, 1948), p. 211.

9. Allan Nevins and John Krout, eds., *The Greater City* (New York: Columbia University Press, 1948), p. 166.

10. Quoted in Arthur F. Burns, *Business Cycle Research and the Needs of our Times,* 33rd Annual Report, National Bureau of Economic Research Inc., 1953, p. 8.

11. Simon Kuznets, *National Income: A Summary of Findings* (New York: National Bureau of Economic Research, 1946), p. 32.

12. Solomon Fabricant, *Output of Manufacturing Industries, 1899–1937* (New York: National Bureau of Economic Research), p. 32.

13. National Industrial Conference Board, *Economic Almanac, 1951–1952* (New York, 1951), p. 92.

14. Raymond G. Goldsmith, *A Study of Saving in the United States* (2 vols.; Princeton University Press, 1955), I, 4.

15. Kuznets, *National Income,* p. 53.

CHAPTER 3. PATTERNS OF CAPITAL AND INDUSTRY

1. Henry Clews, *The Wall Street Point of View* (New York: Silver, Burdett, 1900), p. 4.

2. Andrew W. Mellon, *Taxation, the People's Business* (New York: Macmillan, 1924), p. 28.

3. National Industrial Conference Board, *Economic Almanac 1949–1950* (New York, 1949), p. 320.

4. In 1914 the total value of electrical supplies was under $350,000,000.

5. See William J. Cunningham, "Transportation: Part I, Railways," in *Recent Economic Changes* (2 vols.; New York: McGraw Hill, 1929), vol. I.

6. W. C. Durant persuaded the Du Pont family to buy the Chevrolet Company, and the Chevrolet Company in turn bought control of General Motors.

7. Melvin T. Copeland, "Marketing," in *Recent Economic Changes*, I, 323.

8. *Ibid.*, p. 391.

9. *Detroit News*, November 24, 1922, quoted in Keith Sward, *The Legend of Henry Ford* (New York: Rinehart, 1948), p. 198.

10. Gertrude G. Schroeder, *The Growth of Major Steel Companies, 1900–1950* (Baltimore: Johns Hopkins Press, 1952), p. 197. Of 62 steel-ingot producers listed in 1948, all but 16 had been incorporated before 1906, and one after 1941 (*Ibid.*, p. 201).

11. E. I. Du Pont de Nemours & Company, *Du Pont: The Autobiography of an American Enterprise* (New York: Scribners, 1951), p. 92.

12. William S. Dutton, *Du Pont, 140 Years* (New York: Scribners, 1951), p. 289.

13. Evelyn H. Knowlton, *Pepperell's Progress* (Cambridge: Harvard University Press, 1948), p. 333.

14. Daniel Creamer, *Capital and Output Trends in Manufacturing Industries, 1880–1948*, Occasional Paper No. 41 (New York: National Bureau of Economic Research, 1954), p. 31.

15. *Ibid.*, p. 5.

CHAPTER 4. THE IMPLICATION OF BIG BUSINESS

1. Norman Beasley, *Knudsen: A Biography* (New York: Whittlesey House, 1947), p. 71.

2. Temporary National Economic Committee, *Monograph 13*, Senate Committee Report, 76 Cong., 3 Sess. (Washington: Government Printing Office, 1941), p. 19.

3. People of the State of New York v. North River Sugar Refining Co., 24 NE 834 (1890).

4. State, *ex rel.* v. Standard Oil Co., 49 Ohio 137 (1892); 30 NE 279 (1892).

5. Mark Sullivan, *Our Times* (New York: Scribners, 1927), II, 314.

6. United States v. E. C. Knight Company, 156 U.S. 1 (1895).

7. Theodore Roosevelt, *Autobiography* (New York: Scribners, 1912), p. 427.

8. Addystone Pipe and Steel Co., *et al.*, v. United States, 175 U.S. 211 (1899).

9. Richard Hofstadter in *The Age of Reform* (New York: Knopf, 1955) believes that a "status revolution" had occurred between about 1870 and 1900 in which the old local community leaders, merchants, small manufacturers, and established professional men were superseded in national prestige by the new plutocracy. "They found themselves checked, hampered, and overridden by the agents of the new corporations, the corrupters of legislatures, the buyers of franchises, the allies of the political bosses" (p. 137). While this may have been true, convincing evidence of it has not appeared so far in the writings of businessmen from communities other than the big eastern metropolitan centers.

10. Quoted in William Z. Ripley, ed., *Trusts, Pools and Corporations* (New York: Ginn, 1905), p. 470.

11. T. Roosevelt, *Autobiography*, pp. 429–430.

12. Quoted in Henry R. Seager and Charles A. Gulick, Jr., *Trust and Corporation Problems* (New York: Harpers, 1929), p. 400.

13. *Ibid.*, p. 422.

14. Adolph A. Berle, Jr., and Gardiner C. Means, *The Modern Corporation and Private Property* (New York: Macmillan, 1932), p. 33. The Snyder-Tucker general price index advanced 84 per cent. U.S. Bureau of Census, *Historical Statistics of the United States, 1789–1945* (Washington: Government Printing Office, 1949), p. 231.

15. See Adolph A. Berle, Jr., *The 20th Century Capitalist Revolution* (New York: Harcourt, Brace, 1954).

16. Arthur J. Eddy, *The New Competition* (New York: Appleton, 1912), p. 100.

17. *Iron Age*, February 6, 1908, quoted in Arthur R. Burns, *The Decline of Competition* (New York: McGraw Hill, 1936), p. 79.

18. Isaiah Leo Sharfman, "The Trade Association Movement," *American Economic Review*, 16:I, Supplement (1926), p. 203, quoted in A. R. Burns, *Decline of Competition*, p. 73.

19. Quoted in Frederick Lewis Allen, *Lords of Creation* (New York: Harpers, 1935), p. 280.

20. Quoted in William Z. Ripley, *Main Street and Wall Street* (Boston: Little, Brown, 1927), p. 121.

21. See James Burnham, *The Managerial Revolution* (New York: John Day, 1941) and Oswald Knauth, *Managerial Enterprise* (New York: Norton, 1948.

22. Taylor, *Scientific Management*, pp. 25–26.

23. Selig Perlman in a paper prepared for a meeting of the American Jewish Historical Society, Poughkeepsie, New York, 1954.

24. Testimony of Myron W. Watkins in TNEC, *Monograph 13*, p. 99.

25. Andrew Carnegie, *The Empire of Business* (Garden City: Doubleday, Page, 1902); quotes from pp. 192, 200, 200, 13.

26. C. H. Buford, "How to Become a Railroad President," *What's New*, November 1949, pp. 12–13.

27. Cochran, *Railroad Leaders*, pp. 127–128.

28. Sutton *et al.*, *Business Creed*, p. 55.

29. William H. Henry, "The Business Executive: The Psychodynamics of a Social Role," *American Journal of Sociology*, LIV (January 1949), 287.

30. Herrymon Maurer, *Great Enterprise: Growth and Behavior of the Big Corporation* (New York: Macmillan, 1955), p. 90.

31. *Ibid.*, pp. 90ff.

32. See Peter F. Drucker, *Concept of the Corporation* (New York: John Day, 1946).

33. John L. McCaffrey, "What Corporation Presidents Think about at Night," *Fortune*, September 1953, p. 128.

34. William H. Whyte, Jr., "How Hard Do Executives Work," *Fortune*, January 1954, p. 109.

35. McCaffrey, "Corporation Presidents," pp. 128–140.

36. See National Industrial Conference Board, *Employee Magazines in the United States* (New York, 1925).

37. Sutton *et al.*, *Business Creed*, p. 360.

38. Quoted in Edward L. Bernays, *Public Relations* (Norman: University of Oklahoma Press, 1952), p. 57.

39. See George Creel, *How We Advertised America* (New York: Harpers, 1920).

40. Bernays, *Public Relations*, pp. 87, 91.

41. *Ibid.*, pp. 87–88.

42. N. Danielian, *AT&T* (New York: Vanguard, 1939), p. 302.

43. *Ibid.*, p. 304.

44. See Eric F. Goldman, *Two-Way Street: The Emergence of the Public Relations Counsel* (Boston: Bellman, 1948).

45. Danielian, *AT&T*, pp. 183, 192.

CHAPTER 5. THE ERA OF THE BANKERS

1. Frederick Lewis Allen, *The Great Pierpont Morgan* (New York: Harpers, 1949), p. 251, and Thomas Lamont, *Henry P. Davison* (New York: Harpers, 1933), p. 76.

2. Report of the Committee Appointed to Investigate the Concentration of Control of Money and Credit, *House Report* 1593, 62 Cong., 3 Sess., 1913, p. 89.

3. *Ibid.*, pp. 105–106.

4. Quoted in Alpheus Thomas Mason, *Brandeis — A Free Man's Life* (New York: Viking, 1946), p. 211.

5. O. W. Underwood, *Drifting Sands of Party Politics* (New York: Century, 1928), p. 289.

6. Benjamin Strong, in Edwin W. Kemmerer, *"The ABC of the Federal Reserve System* (Princeton: Princeton University Press, 1918), p. ix.

7. Hearings on the Banking Act of 1935, Senate Committee on Banking and Currency, p. 406, quoted from Hermann Krooss, "Business Opinion between Two Wars: An Analysis of Statements of Business Leaders on Economic Issues" (Ph.D. Thesis, New York University, 1948), p. 54.

8. H. G. S. Noble, "The New York Stock Exchange in the Crisis of 1914," quoted in Humphrey B. Neill, *The Inside Story of the Stock Exchange* (New York: B. C. Forbes, 1950), p. 191.

9. Paul M. Mazur, *American Prosperity* (New York: Viking, 1928), p. 250.

10. Quoted in Allen, *Lords of Creation*, p. 335.

11. See Ripley, *Main Street and Wall Street*, pp. 330ff.

12. Quoted in Broadus Mitchell, *Depression Decade* (New York: Rinehart, 1947), p. 163.

13. Burns, *Business Cycle Research*, p. 4.

14. James D. Richardson, ed., *A Compilation of the Messages and Papers of the Presidents* (Washington: Government Printing Office, 1898), IX, 390.

15. "Everybody Ought to be Rich," *Ladies' Home Journal*, XLIV (August 1929), 299, quoted in John A. Penrod, "The Literature of the Great Depression" (Ph.D. Thesis, University of Pennsylvania, 1954), p. 58.

CHAPTER 6. BUSINESS IN STAGNATION AND BOOM

1. *Time*, July 9, 1956, p. 74.

2. *Economic Almanac, 1951–1952*, p. 203. The 1928 figure is estimated.

3. Kuznets, *National Income*, p. 32.

4. *Economic Almanac, 1951–1952*, p. 203.

5. See Goldsmith, *A Study of Saving*, vol. 1, chap. i.

6. For composite chart made up from the figures of various government agencies, see George Soule, *Economic Forces in American History* (New York: William Sloan, 1952), p. 246.

7. Arthur F. Burns, *Looking Forward*, 31st Annual Report, National Bureau of Economic Research (New York, 1951), p. 4, based on research by Simon Kuznets.

8. Leonard P. Ayres, chart published by Cleveland Trust Company, Cleveland, Ohio, 1942 (later editions available).

9. Herbert Hoover, *Memoirs of Herbert Hoover: The Great Depression, 1929–1941* (New York: Macmillan, 1952), p. 2.

10. Samuel L. Clemens, *Mark Twain in Eruption*, edited by Bernard DeVoto (New York: Harpers, 1940), p. 17.

11. Paul W. Litchfield, *Industrial Voyage* (New York: Doubleday, 1954), p. 254.

12. Quoted in Richard Hofstadter, *The American Political Tradition* (New York: Knopf, 1948), p. 325.

13. *Ibid.*, p. 326.

14. The argument as stated here is condensed with minor changes from Arthur F. Burns, *The Instability of Consumer Spending*, 32nd Annual Report, National Bureau of Economic Research (New York, 1952).

15. John M. Keynes, *The General Theory of Employment, Interest and Money* (New York: Harcourt, Brace, 1936), p. 320.

16. *Ibid.*, p. 96.

17. Kuznets, *National Income*, p. 99.

18. Simon Kuznets, "Economic Growth and Income Inequality," *American Economic Review*, XLV (March 1955), 7.

19. Harold G. Moulton, *Formation of Capital* (Washington: Brookings Institution, 1935), pp. 158–159.

20. *Historical Statistics of U.S., 1789–1945*, pp. 67, 68 for wages; p. 235 for price indices.

21. Moulton, *Formation of Capital*, p. 145.

22. Specifically, 11.9 per cent of total income in 1929; 15.1 per cent in 1950 (Burns, *Consumer Spending*, p. 19).

23. Leo Grebler, *The Role of Federal Credit Aids in Residential Construction* (New York: National Bureau of Economic Research, 1953), p. 4.

24. Burns, *Consumer Spending*, p. 18.

25. *Ibid., passim.*

26. *Time*, October 18, 1954, p. 94.

CHAPTER 7. A NEW BUSINESS ENVIRONMENT

1. *Time*, March 15, 1954, p. 100.

2. Grosvenor B. Clarkson, *Industrial America in the World War* (Boston: Houghton Mifflin, 1923), p. 233.

3. *Ibid.*, p. 235.

4. *Historical Statistics of the U. S.*, p. 65.

5. Quoted in Eliot Janeway, *The Struggle for Survival* (New Haven: Yale University Press, 1950), p. 72.

6. *Ibid.*, p. 83.

7. Beasley, *Knudsen*, p. 322.

8. Donald M. Nelson, *Arsenal of Democracy* (New York: Harcourt, Brace, 1946), p. 224.

9. *Ibid.*, p. 212.

10. Frederic C. Lane, *Ships for Victory* (Baltimore: Johns Hopkins University Press, 1951), p. 5.

11. Courtney R. Hall, *History of American Industrial Science* (New York: Science Library Publishers, 1954), p. 414.

## CHAPTER 8. BUSINESS AND THE PUBLIC

1. Hoover, *The Great Depression*, p. 97.

2. Krooss, "American Business Opinion," pp. 119ff.

3. Franklin D. Roosevelt, *Public Papers and Addresses*, II, 11ff.

4. Quoted in Hofstadter, *American Political Tradition*, p. 329n.

5. Schechter Corp. v. United States, 295 U.S. 495 (1935).

6. Franklin D. Roosevelt, Message to World Economic Conference, London, 1933.

7. Herbert Hoover, *The Challenge to Liberty*, quoted in E. C. Rozwenc, ed., *The New Deal*, Amherst College Series (Boston: D. C. Heath, 1949), p. 70.

8. Report of the President, New York Stock Exchange, August 11, 1937, quoted in Neill, *Inside Story of Stock Exchange*, pp. 257–258.

9. Miles L. Colean, *The Impact of Government on Real Estate Finance in the United States* (New York: National Bureau of Economic Research, 1950), pp. 94–99.

10. *Senate Report* 6, 76 Cong., 1 Sess., part 6, Report of the Committee on Education and Labor, pp. 42–43.

11. Testimony of Robert B. Henderson, Vice-President, National Association of Manufacturers, *ibid.*, p. 44.

12. Hoover, *The Great Depression*, pp. 433–434.

13. Eric F. Goldman, *Rendezvous with Destiny* (New York: Knopf, 1952), p. 365.

14. The N.L.R.B. v. Jones and Laughlin Corp., 301 U.S. 1 (1937).

15. Quoted in Bernays, *Public Relations*, p. 104.

16. General Electric Company *Employee Relations News Letter*, January 7, 1953.

17. Quoted in Eugene Staley, ed., *Creating an Industrial Civili-*

*zation: A Report of the Corning Conference* (New York: Harpers, 1952), p. 143.

18. Bernays, *Public Relations,* p. 108.

19. Joe S. Bain, "Industrial Concentration and Anti-Trust Policy," in Harold F. Williamson, ed., *Growth of American Economy* (New York: Prentice-Hall, 1951), p. 879.

20. Quoted in Charles R. Whittlesey, *National Interest and International Cartels* (New York: Macmillan, 1946), p. 6.

21. A. D. H. Kaplan, *Big Enterprise in a Competitive System* (Washington: Brookings Institution, 1954), p. 31.

22. *Time,* December 10, 1951, p. 91.

23. Sidney Fine, *Laissez-Faire and the General Welfare State* (Ann Arbor: University of Michigan Press, 1956), p. 399.

24. E. Pendleton Herring, *Public Administration and Public Interest* (New York: McGraw Hill, 1936), p. 173.

25. *Fortune,* May 1949, p. 67.

26. *Look,* February 8, 1955, pp. 19–20.

CHAPTER 9.  AMERICAN BUSINESSMEN

1. See Kaplan, *Big Enterprise in a Competitive System,* pp. 231–241.

2. U.S. Chamber of Commerce, *Survey of Current Business* (Washington: Government Printing Office, 1949), p. 10.

3. This and other Southwestern interview material is the result of a trip taken for this purpose in 1950, made possible by grants from the American Philosophical Society and the University of Pennsylvania.

4. TNEC, *Monograph 17,* p. 91.

5. *Ibid.,* pp. 81–86.

6. Sidney Goldstein and Kurt Mayer, "Patterns of Business Growth and Survival in a Medium-Sized Community," *Journal of Economic History,* XVII (June 1957), 193–206.

7. TNEC, *Monograph 17,* p. 230.

8. Atherton, *Main Street on the Middle Border,* pp. 339–340.

9. XIT Ranch Papers, Panhandle-Plains Historical Museum, Canyon, Texas.

10. F. W. Taussig and C. S. Joslyn, *American Business Leaders* (New York: Macmillan, 1932).

11. W. Lloyd Warner and James C. Abegglen, *Occupational Mobility in American Business and Industry, 1928–1952* (Minneapolis: University of Minnesota Press, 1955), p. 229.

12. Mabel Newcomer, "The Chief Executive of Large Business Corporations," *Explorations in Entrepreneurial History* (October 1952), pp. 13–14.

13. *Boston Sunday Herald,* December 12, 1948.

14. Carl D. Thompson, *Confessions of the Power Trust* (New York: Dutton, 1932), p. 14.

15. Knauth, *Managerial Enterprise,* p. 28.

16. See Danielian, *AT&T,* pp. 102–103; and Arthur A. Bright, Jr., *The Electric-Lamp Industry* (New York: Macmillan, 1949), pp. 384–391. Paul G. Clark, in *Structure of the American Economy,* Wassily Leontief, ed. (2nd ed.; New York: Oxford University Press, 1951) pictures the investment policy of AT&T as a kind of automatic adjustment to new demand on a basis worked out by engineers. Entrepreneurial decisions do not appear explicitly.

17. Knauth, *Managerial Enterprise,* pp. 45, 46.

18. Peter F. Drucker, *The Practice of Management* (New York: Harpers, 1954), p. 132.

19. David Riesman, *From Conspicuous Consumption to Conspicuous Production* (Glencoe, Illinois: The Free Press, 1954), pp. 224–225.

20. *Fortune,* May 1954, p. 117.

21. Warner and Abegglen, *Occupational Mobility,* p. 45.

22. Sutton *et al., Business Creed,* pp. 3ff.

23. *Ibid.,* p. 285.

24. *Ibid.,* pp. 251–262.

CHAPTER 10. CULTURAL CHANGE AND CHALLENGE

1. "The Changing Character of Business," *World's Work,* June 1926, quoted in Krooss, "American Business Opinion," p. 22.

2. James W. Prothero, *The Dollar Decade: Business Ideas in the 1920's* (Baton Rouge: Louisiana State University Press, 1954), p. 236.

3. *Ibid.,* pp. 209–210.

4. Quoted in Krooss, "American Business Opinion," p. 149.

5. *New York Times,* June 7, 1932, quoted in Krooss, "American Business Opinion," p. 121.

6. "Report of Seminar on American Values" (mimeographed, University of Pennsylvania, 1955).

7. John K. Jessup, "A Political Role for the Corporation," *Fortune,* August 1952, p. 113.

8. Riesman, *From Conspicuous Consumption to Conspicuous Production,* pp. 224–225.

9. Quoted in A. R. Raskin, "The Corporation on the Campus," *New York Times Magazine,* April 17, 1955, p. 63.

10. Jessup, "A Political Role for the Corporation," p. 156.

11. Quoted in Staley, *Creating an Industrial Civilization,* pp. 204–205.

12. Macmillan, 1933. See also Alexander R. Heron, *Why Men Work* (Stanford: Stanford University Press, 1948).

13. *Time*, April 14, 1952, p. 97.

14. Edward C. Bursk, "Introduction," *Human Relations for Management* (New York: Harpers, 1956), a collection of articles from the *Harvard Business Review*, 1950–1955.

15. Quoted in Staley, *Creating an Industrial Civilization*, p. 204.

16. These values or beliefs have been suggested by the analyses of anthropolgists and sociologists. While no formal consensus has been attempted, I have never come across basic opposition to the formulations given here. See Clyde Kluckhohn, *Mirror for Man: The Relation of Anthropology to Modern Life* (New York: Whittlesey House, 1949), p. 232; Robin W. Williams, Jr., *American Society: A Sociological Interpretation* (New York: Knopf, 1951), pp. 441–442; and F. L. K. Hau, "Culture Factors," *Factors in Economic Development: Principles and Patterns,* edited by Harold F. Williamson and John A. Buttrick (New York: Prentice-Hall, 1954), pp. 340–341.

17. Merle E. Curti, "Intellectuals and Other People," *American Historical Review,* LX (January 1955), p. 265.

18. Bernays, *Public Relations,* chap. xxxiii.

19. Matthew Josephson, in *The Nation* January 14, 1956, pp. 30–33; January 21, 1956, pp. 50–52; January 28, 1956, pp. 69–72. C. Wright Mills, *The Power Elite* (New York: Oxford Press, 1956).

20. *Fortune,* May 1949; see also Elmo Roper, "The Public Looks at Business," *Harvard Business Review,* May 1949, p. 165.

21. Marquis W. Childs and Douglas Cater, *Ethics in a Business Society* (New York: New American Library of World Literature, 1954), p. 176.

22. Quoted in Staley, *Creating an Industrial Civilization,* p. 174.

# Index

Abegglen, J. C., 178, 184
Abrams, Frank, quoted, 137, 195
Accounting, 52, 69, 73
Adams, Brooks, 9, 10
Adams, Franklin P., 66
Adams, Henry, 9, 29
Addystone Pipe Case, 54
Administration. *See* Management
Advertising, 40, 130, 155, 157.
  *See also* Public relations
Africa, 6, 171
Agricultural Adjustment Act
  (AAA), *1933*, 144, 146
Agriculture. *See* Farmers
Airplane, 14, 44–45, 132–134
Alcott, Bronson, 10
Aldrich, Winthrop D., quoted, 89
Allen, Frederick Lewis, quoted,
  155
Amarillo, 174, 176
American Farm Bureau Federa-
  tion, 150
*American Magazine,* 140
American Telephone & Telegraph
  Co., 31, 65, 73, 77–78, 181–182
American Tobacco Co., 67
Amsterdam, 81
Appersons, the, 36
Arnold, Thurman W., 158
Asia, 6
Atherton, Lewis, quoted, 5, 7, 171
Atlantic City, 143
Atomic energy, 107, 138, 161
Atomic Energy Commission, 138
Autocar Co., 42
Automobiles: busses, 42–43, 124,

128, 131–132; industry, 13, 18–
19, 21, 33–49, 123–128, 135–
136; trucks, 14, 42–43, 121,
124, 131–132, 136. *See also* individual companies
Avery, C. W., 39
Ayres, C. E., quoted, 16

Baker, George F., 81–86; quoted,
  85
Balchen, Bert, 45
Baltimore, 139
Bankers. *See* Banking
Bankers Trust Co., 82, 84
Banking, 82–96, 141–149, 174–
176; investment, vii, 79–89,
97–98
Banks. *See* Banking
Barton, Bruce, 140
Baruch, Bernard, 143; quoted,
  135, 180
Batten, A. H., quoted, 155
Bell, Alexander Graham, 31
Bell System, 77. *See also* Amer-
  ican Telephone & Telegraph
  Co.
Belmont, August, & Co., 84
Berle, Adolph A., Jr., 59–60
Berlin, 81
Bernays, Edward L., 77; quoted,
  156, 200
Bessemer process, 45
Bethlehem Steel Co., 46
Beveridge, Albert, quoted, 10
Bicycle, 36
Boston, 31, 128

219